FLATPACK DEMOCRACY

A DIY GUIDE TO CREATING INDEPENDENT POLITICS

BY

PETER MACFADYEN

eco-logic books

First published in 2014 by eco-logic books. Reprinted 2016 and 2017.
www.eco-logicbooks.com

ISBN 978 1899233 22 9

Cover Design	Matt Wellsted	**www.thedraughtsman.me**
Book Design	Steve Palmer	**www.thedesigncoop.co.uk**
Printed by	Russell Press on 100% recycled paper	**www.russellpress.com**

Further copies of this book may be bought from eco-logic books. We would welcome enquiries for bulk orders of this book from independent local groups.

Contents

1. Foreword

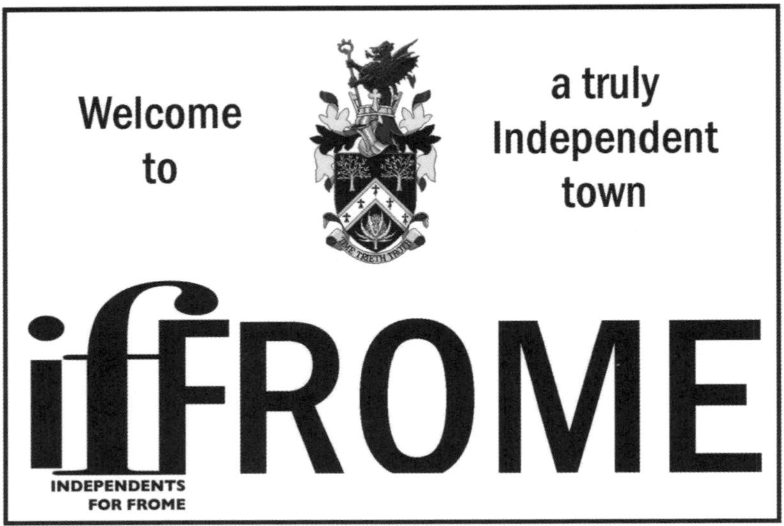

This book was written as a guide to taking political power at local level. It will also set out some ideas as to how that power can be used to enable people to have a greater say in the things that are important to them. It is based on what happened here in Frome, so it is both an instruction manual and a history.

Although some of my fellow councillors have commented on early drafts, this guide is an independent creation and I am entirely responsible for the contents, views and mistakes.

My start point is the crisis in democracy in Great Britain. I would suggest that the problem is not the people – who are as keen to be involved as ever – but the systems for governance and our democratic structures that are manifestly no longer fit for purpose.

This work proposes an approach that aims to bring about change from within. It recognises that there are many politicians who have served with dedication for years and have done so with the best of intent. But that now they may need to step aside or embrace new ways of working.

It is primarily aimed at local levels of governance – though the principles and underlying ethos apply throughout the UK's political system and beyond. It is based on the experiences of a group of individuals who came together in Frome in 2011 to replace the party politicians who made up the town council.

In our experience, at local levels of representation, party politics as practiced by the current political parties are an irrelevant and corrosive diversion. A diversion which critically reduces the pool of people prepared to serve as councillors. The people who formed Independents for Frome (IfF) came together because they cared about their local community and wished to focus solely on bringing benefit to Frome. We developed a Way of Working which is not simply to form another party. Our intention was not to replace one set of individuals struggling within the system with another, but to try and invent a process that would drag local decision making into the 21st century. Within IfF we maintain that 'Yes' is a better answer than 'No'; that the possibility of making mistakes should be encouraged; that diversity and different views are positive; and that community leadership is about making bold, local decisions.

What we are doing in Frome is attempting to create a new, inclusive democracy, starting from the grassroots up. We've only just begun this process and have succeeded in only some areas. As far as possible, this guide draws on parallel experiences taking place in other parts of the country. The associated blog and website will pick up on 'what happened next' and add learning from others.

We have set out to encourage and inform those who wish to attempt a similar journey. We do not yet know if the story of one dynamic parish council can be replicated, nor whether Frome can spark a national movement for change – questions I will return to in the final chapter.

What is clear, though, is that change is essential. As Albert Einstein said: "the definition of insanity is doing the same thing over and over again and expecting different results."

2. Democracy in Crisis

Britain today operates a dysfunctional political system. Many of those making decisions do so to meet their own or their political parties' needs, not those of the people they serve. The quest for power reduces both creativity and relevance, especially at local level. Systems of government, developed years ago, are largely not suited to the age we live in, restricting both elected representatives and civil servants. These factors combine to turn the vast majority of people away from engagement in politics, which in turn leads to negativity, cynicism and a greater risk of social unrest. With too few people engaged in the decision-making processes, politicians become unrepresentative of the public at large and more vulnerable to manipulation.

Fewer people are engaged in local decision-making.

Over the last 50 years the number of people voting in national elections has fallen from around 80% to around 60%. At local levels of government fewer and fewer people vote, and those that do are becoming increasingly elderly. Around 40% vote in local and 30% in European elections. A mere 15% voted for their Police Commissioners – significantly fewer votes cast than in many TV talent shows.

With a lower turnout, democracy becomes meaningless. For example, I was elected to Frome Town Council with 365 votes. So, of the voters I represent, around 90% didn't vote for me. In many local elections a handful of voters effectively make the decision. In general, politicians are speaking to each other and to a tiny number of people who are prepared to engage. The Liberal Democrat candidate in a recent Wigan by-election managed to get just 19 votes.

There are also fewer people prepared to put themselves forward as candidates, especially at local level. This frequently results in council seats not being contested. For example, in the May 2013 elections, in 16 parishes in the Marlborough area, only one had enough candidates for an election, and in one case there were no candidates at all. Across England, the same 2013 local elections saw 1,200 people (59% of all seats) being elected unopposed. In the most recent district elections in 24 local authorities, at least one in ten councillors, were appointed unopposed. The worst offender was Eden District Council in Cumbria, where exactly half of all councillors took their seats uncontested.

Another example is East Dorset District Council where one third of candidates were 'elected' without opposition.

Cynicism runs so deep that comedian Russell Brand is campaigning to 'completely renounce the current paradigm' based on fellow comedian Billy Connolly's comments: "Don't vote, it encourages them" and "The desire to be a politician should bar you for life from ever being one." His plea not to vote had over ten million viewers on YouTube the following week after an initial TV interview – coverage no politician can ever hope to achieve.

> "Aren't you bored, aren't you more bored than anyone? Ain't you been talking to [politicians] year after year, listening to their lies, their nonsense, then it's this one gets in, that one gets in, but the problem continues? Why are we going to continue to contribute to that facade?"
>
> *Newsnight interview, Russell Brand speaking to Jeremy Paxman.*

The System is unrepresentative.

This systematic lack of engagement is further exacerbated by our 'first past the post' system. In most UK general elections the winning party has around 30% support and all the power. Many people's views are not represented at all, or are represented poorly. According to Wikipedia, in the national elections of 2010, for example, 900,000 UKIP and 550,000 BNP voters gained no representation, 265,000 voters lead to the one Green MP, and yet an average of 35,000 voters provided each Conservative MP. With the steady creep of party politics to local levels, this dominance of the victors entrenches a massively non-representative minority. For example, at Mendip District Council the 31 Conservatives exert total control over their 16 opposition councillors despite the fact that the majority of voters either did not vote, or voted something other than Conservative.

In addition, because most people do what they always did, in only a tiny number of seats is it likely or possible to bring about change. So much so that in the last national election, in 30% of all seats, no money at all was spent by any candidate on public meetings – why bother? The Electoral Reform Society tells us that total spend over the UK ranges from 14p per voter to over £3.00 depending on how much your vote is worth.

At a national level we see the House of Commons largely made up of men and headed by millionaires – 23 out of 27 of the current coalition cabinet, apparently – which is hardly representative of the population at large. While two thirds of Rwandan MPs are women and Sweden manages nearly half, the UK has less than a quarter, with only five in a cabinet recently described as overwhelmingly 'Male, Pale and Stale'. Given that enthusiasm for voting is directly related to whether you think your vote will lead to change, is it any wonder that cynicism and disengagement is fast becoming endemic?

However, once elected, no political party is brave enough or moral enough to legislate for a fairer system. The current system worked for them but a more equable system might not. So they vigorously block change. Witness the debacle in 2011, when the proposed change to a slightly more representative system was faced with the full destructive might of the major political parties and their press backers. So desperate were the Liberal Democrats to achieve a system that would benefit them that they caved in on a range of issues previously held dear, only then to be sold down the river by their Tory coalition partners.

Finally, too few people voting for too few candidates risks some outlandish and – in my view – dangerous people taking power. High on my list would be

Northern Ireland's current Minister of Health Edwin Poots, who was elected having been First Preference for under 5% of those registered to vote in Lagan Valley. Mr Poots is a 'young-earth creationist' who believes the earth began 4,000 years ago. A worrying viewpoint for someone in a ministerial position which, perhaps more than most, should include an ability to rationally assess evidence.

How could it get worse? Political parties.

When most people stand for election they stand as a representative of a political party. What you can find out about your candidate focuses on the party they represent, not on who they are. Little, if anything, is known about themselves, their beliefs, interests, affiliations, skills or background. The party will have a manifesto or a set of promises which has little or no relevance at local level. And, as we have seen, at national level many promises are never implemented or are later rejected. Just one sad example would be the Liberal Democrats, who had a signed manifesto promise not to increase tuition fees and then supported increases once in coalition with the Conservatives.

Once elected, individual representatives are expected to follow the line they are given by those in a far flung 'Central Office', the Cabinet, or the leadership group. This adherence to ideology and the party line strangles engagement and reduces the capacity to make good decisions. Nowhere is this clearer than at local levels. My experience of party politics has been farcical. In Frome the Tories, as a group, are constrained by their nationally dictated ideology of austerity. This means almost all recommendations to spend or borrow are rejected, whether budgeted for or not. Indeed, they almost always vote against everything, memorably including: "I don't understand this so I am voting against it on principle." Voting as a group, where ideology has priority over individual knowledge and understanding drastically reduces the usefulness of all party councillors. This behaviour also introduces an undercurrent of negativity whereby irrespective of personal views, the evidence before them, whether the issue is actually a good idea or not you vote against whatever the other lot are voting for. To the watching public this behaviour is baffling and farcical.

Of course there are good councils and good councillors, and at higher levels it would be much more difficult to reach a decision without a known degree of support from colleagues. To many it no longer makes any sense that councillors are elected just because they have a link to an ideology that has little relevance at local level and a set of promises which are frequently broken.

Party politics has a further hugely debilitating feature that candidates must be party members. As membership of any political party plummets, the potential pool for selection is getting even smaller. For example in Frome none of the main parties could find 17 candidates to contest all the seats at the last town elections. If you couple this with internal squabbles it can well lead to some truly appalling choices. We have seen how internal political battles take time and energy away from dealing with issues, as do the endless meetings and conferences associated with party membership. Ultimately, party politicians are often torn between what is best for the community and answering to their party leadership and ideology, with the latter winning out far too often.

As if all that wasn't bad enough, bring on the rules, conventions and language.

To compound this travesty, the rules under which councils and parliaments operate were often devised in and for a different age. At a national level, in Westminster, we see two sets of rich men shout at each other in puerile, point scoring, public school style 'debates', with planted questions and prepared answers. We see party Whips make sure MPs vote the party way, and a minefield of rules and regulations around member's bills, the Queen's speech and the whole panoply of parliamentary procedure. And as if that weren't enough, we have an unelected House of Lords that can veto and hold up legislation.

[As an aside, notes and letters written at the time of the shaping of the American Constitution make it perfectly clear that the powerful men of the time were deliberately devising a system so complex that it could not be threatened by democracy. Why should this surprise us? If everyone was truly represented in the UK, the tiny minority of rich males who currently dominate our decision making would be hardly visible.]

At the local level of democracy, when I was a town councillor in Lostwithiel (co-opted in as no-one stood), it took me about two years to understand the protocol. "...I'm sorry councillor Macfadyen, you were not standing when you made that point, but it will come around next year." In Frome my first question as a new councillor was "who are the 'members'?" The answer (with smirks from the old hands) was "you are". No one told me councillors are called 'members' (and the staff are called 'officers').

This assumption that everyone understands the rules and language makes it incredibly hard for newcomers to raise issues. For example, new Independent councillor Simon Carter (of Just Tewksbury) found himself thrown into the selection of committee members at the first meeting with no information on what the committees did, let alone attempts to link expertise with posts. Baffled by the confidence of old hands, decisions were instantly made which then couldn't easily be changed.

The culture seems to be 'let's start off by publicly embarrassing those who don't understand the system and then exclude those who don't understand the language'. That leaves those who have mastered the jargon and understand the rules to control what's discussed. And where is the public in all this? They left long ago in total confusion.

And then there are the staff...

Being involved in politics I can also see that not only is the system dysfunctional in how we elect our representatives but also in relation to the people who either choose or are forced to work for them. At the higher levels of government, I suspect the Sir Humphrey character is more than just a dramatic invention and that civil servants can get away with non compliance by hiding behind a smoke screen of inactivity and subterfuge. This leaves their political masters confused and ineffective.

As an extreme example, I know of a chief executive who apparently spent significant amounts of time investigating complaints by the public in relation to the councillors' behaviour. None of these could ever be revealed 'because of confidentiality', but the constant threat of exposure left new councillors nervous and clearly showed where the power lay.

The paid staff often have to work with ongoing confusion. Every four years policy, strategy, structures and jobs are all likely to change. Every few weeks they are asked to present papers to ministers, councillors and the public which are then often ridiculed and rejected. The public blame them for everything and applaud them for nothing. Of course there are exceptions, but once again we have set up a system in which it is hard to see how the best can be drawn from staff. All too often the only way they can effectively run their council or department is to hoard knowledge, squirrel away information and only concede power when forced to. Yet again democracy and engagement lose out.

So what will happen without change?

This is the system we've got. The main argument – that we should retain it because it has fewer faults than others – is a lazy one and hugely risky. As cynicism increases and more people turn away from rational argument, they often turn to the politics of extremism: witness the rise of the Golden Dawn in Greece and UKIP in the UK. We are nurturing an environment where social unrest is inevitable. This may be at a low level, undermining safety and wellbeing, or a full blown 'Arab Spring' where the old order is violently swept away. More immediately, the current system is not a fertile one in which to nurture community engagement, develop greater participation and strengthen community resilience. It's a system of missed opportunity which fails to draw in the many, talented people who'd love to play a bigger part in decision making in their community.

3. Why Bother?

IfF campaign leaflet

So far I have described a political system which I believe is increasingly dysfunctional. Indeed, I may well have persuaded you that you do not want to have anything to do with such a depressing scenario. However, gird your loins, for from here on I want to make the case for change.

I believe we do not have to wait for collapse or revolution. We have the tools to create a better model, using real democracy, to bring about change from within. This means firstly taking power, then, as quickly as possible, changing the basic systems to make them more open and engaging. Finding ways to turn the role of the council from service provider to enabler. Engaging with a majority of people to bring them into the decision making process. So, if you are still up for the challenge, here are some questions you might want to ask:

1. Why is now the moment to get involved?
2. Why Independent?
3. Why you?
4. What do you hope to achieve?
5. How much does it cost?
6. How much of time will it take?
7. Is it worth it?

Why now?

The failures of our current democratic systems, amply outlined above, aren't new. Any two people sitting in a pub will quickly point them out to you. However, especially at the local levels of representation, three new factors have emerged that will aid those seeking fundamental change in grassroots politics:

1) The underemployed and the unemployed

Historically many parish and town councillors have been drawn from three groups:

- Elderly and retired people with good local knowledge, time and commitment but not necessarily any wider skills in – for example – budgeting, public engagement or managing people.
- Younger professionals with political aspirations.
- Local business people, especially property developers and landowners with clear personal experience and interest.

In Paul Mason's book *Twenty Reasons why it's Kicking off Everywhere* he quotes a historian of the French Revolution of 1789 as saying 'significant change is usually not the product of poor people but of poor lawyers'. At the heart of the uprisings in North Africa and recent unrest in Spain and Greece have been unemployed young people and recent graduates. In the UK too, there is a vast pool of young unemployed and underemployed people who could be drawn into local politics if they saw a reason so to be.

Personally, I'm writing this in a period of self-unemployment while a new funeral business takes off and my consultancy work with Comic Relief has a year's compulsory holiday. In my case, being a councillor is not a career move – I may not stand again after this four year period. Like being a school governor, or a charity trustee, it can be a way of engaging in a community and really making a difference. A key difference for an Independent is that they can focus on community good rather than getting embroiled in party issues. There is no greasy political pole to climb.

Fewer and fewer people have full time work and an increasing number work from home – perfect material for local councillors. Plus if decision making at a local level were to become more inspiring, more enjoyable and crucially actually lead to change, I am certain a greater pool of people will want to engage. In addition supporters who can give smaller or irregular amounts of time and expertise would have a valued role.

2) New media

The second key factor is social media and the Internet. New ways to contact people, network, engage, annoy and influence emerge every day. When new ideas arise they can be quickly 'market tested'. Then they take off, bubble under or disappear. The 'archetypal' protest leader, organiser, facilitator, spokesperson is now, more often than not, an educated young woman with a knowledge of how to exploit the Internet. Suddenly political involvement can move geographically (electronically) from a small community to international issues. For example Avaaz – a 'global web movement to bring people-powered politics to decision making everywhere' – has more than 21 million members. If that many people email a government to protest an issue, at the very least it lets them know they aren't operating in secret.

Italian standup comedian Beppe Grillo's M5S party recently won almost a quarter of the general election votes spending nothing on traditional media advertising. And after a series of successes in 16 different countries, Pirate Parties International (which "...strives to reveal the impact of multinational trade agreements on all people on earth, and foster freedom and democracy...") is run over the Internet with part time workers.

At a local level political engagement may be something as simple as a dedicated Facebook group. In Frome there is one such group currently putting the spotlight on dog mess. They have come up with a raft of new ideas and actions to tackle something local politics has failed to deal with for years. This speed of dissemination of ideas over a range of new media options is key for new movements as they seek to take power. Once in control it can also be a vital tool in adjusting policy and really engaging with the community on a regular basis.

3) Localism

In the Coalition Agreement of May 2010 the Prime Minister and Deputy Prime Minister said "The time has come to disperse power more widely in Britain today." 'Localism' and the 'Big Society' set out to give significant decision making to people at a community level. For once I may not be cynical enough, but I still believe the Localism Act does try to address the key issue of power devolution. I agree with Susan Fainstein when she said that ".... at the level of the neighbourhood, there is the greatest opportunity for democracy but the least amount of power. As we scale up, the amount of decision making power increases but the potential of people to affect outcomes diminishes."

The Act does give powers to local communities BUT there are key challenges as to what 'local' means. For us in Frome, all too often we have found it means 'district' and with an uncooperative and highly politicised district, the potential of the Act has not yet been achieved. Worryingly, as the economy splutters out of recession (possibly temporarily) Localism is no longer a priority for government whereas many would claim it is exactly that flowering of creativity, at local level, that will drive the next wave of employment.

However, the essence of Localism underpins the ethos of the coup we orchestrated in Frome and is a key driver for the rest of this guide. The case I aim to establish is that it is worth the effort of taking power because you can elicit real change. Frome is a frontrunner in creating a Neighbourhood Plan – a key element in Localism – and in other ways we are using the positive aspects of the new Act as they emerge. Without this Act, it would be even more difficult for a town or parish council to engender real change.

> "Congratulations… the Big Society"
> *Tory to IfF tweet on election day.*

In addition Localism also allows the interesting option of creating a truly local council if you are in a city where this doesn't exist. In early 2012 Queen's Park residents in north Westminster voted 'yes' in a referendum to decide whether to establish a community council, better known as a parish council. The council will be London's first new parish council since 1963, when parishes were abolished to make way for the Greater London Council. They are now engaged in the interesting question as to whether the (non party) group that orchestrated this change will find themselves ousted by local party politicians in the election of representatives.

Why Independent?

I have already covered the disadvantages of political parties in local politics. Without these constraints Independents can put the needs of their community first. In addition, not being driven by a primary concern of gaining and keeping power is massively liberating. Independence allows a greater degree of risk taking. This is something I believe is increasingly valuable in a changing world, a world where it is important to adapt quickly in order to seize new opportunities. Generally I am an advocate for the strongest possible engagement with the public to seek their views. However, there will be times when Independent councillors need to listen, then boldly make their own decisions. Without the constraints of party doctrine and fear around retaining power, this is much more likely to happen.

> At the start of the IfF adventure we shared this with the public: "We don't intend to be around forever. Community movements like ours can emerge, be effective, do whatever is necessary and then step down gracefully. Time marches on and we don't necessarily intend to ask for public support beyond the next four years. None of us feel the need to hang onto power and we have no party machine that needs feeding with new candidates or indeed recycling the old. Perhaps if we get some things right other Independents will emerge during our time in office and they will step into our shoes, who knows?"

Local councillors are volunteers. It is important that their interests are allowed to blossom, to be used and appreciated, both to get the best use of their skills and to build engagement. I believe people are more likely to give time and enthusiasm to things they know, care about and that directly affect them. Independence allows for these factors to be more easily recognised and acted on. The fact that representatives at higher levels are paid brings its own problems as the money can influence motivation rather than the desire to engage.

A group of Independents also has another much underestimated strength – diversity. There is great strength to be found in recognising and appreciating differences while working to common aims. Within IfF we have found that our common aims far outweigh any differences. As Independents we are working exclusively for the best for our community. Most of the time we'll agree; much of the time we'll recognise someone else's greater expertise; and occasionally we either agree to disagree, or recognise it's not important. By their very nature, political parties demand a uniformity of views and opinions from their members and therefore they miss out on the richness diversity brings. A group of Independents will bring to the table a range of views and experiences that better reflects the wider society in which they live.

When IfF started in Frome I, in my red shoes and baggy jersey, had never previously met Nick White, in his smart jacket, tie and expensive shoes. Nick's partner said "Nick White and Peter Macfadyen in one room – it will never work." We have fundamental disagreements on a whole range of issues, but so far we've enjoyed the difference. I believe it has been good for Frome and enriching for both of us.

Why you?

Firstly, why would you consider becoming a politician? Traditionally people enter politics for a variety of reasons: a desire to put something back into their community; a belief in the ideology of a party; a platform for a personal political career; ego and personal gain through influence in planning and other decision making.

This is a generally depressing list with the exception of the first reason. However, I believe working as an Independent within a group of Independents is a real opportunity for individuals to work together to fundamentally change the way our communities work and to bring real benefits to their own community. Sadly there will still be career politicians and corrupt egoists (are they the same?) but perhaps we can marginalise them by sheer numbers of committed and motivated activists?

My personal motivation for standing as a councillor was around environmental issues. With a background of work on climate change, I am convinced that we need to radically and speedily reduce our impact on the planet. In common with the Transition Towns movement, I believe we need to build resilient communities able to cope with the shocks ahead. Much of this interest is now reflected in council policy and actions on energy, ethics, moving to a One Planet Frome and building a more participative community.

Secondly there are questions to ask before considering coming forward: what are your aspirations? Do you seek marginal improvement or a paradigm shift? Asking these will help you decide whether the effort ahead will be worth it. Instigating significant change at all levels takes time and energy, so you will need to realistically estimate how much effort you are prepared to put in. Let's look specifically at some important questions:

What do you want to achieve?

My view is: be ambitious. Be part of a movement that stands in every seat. Go for power. Who wants to spend four years rearranging the political deckchairs on a council *Titanic*. If all you are going to do is simply replace one set of ineffective councillors, operating in a dysfunctional system, with another, why bother?

I would suggest that unless you are motivated by creating a society that is more able to face the future and believe the council exists to empower the wider community rather than to direct it, then stick to the day job.

Martin Seligman, in his book *Flourish* shows functioning societies have five key elements:

1. People feel good about themselves
2. They are deeply engaged in activity
3. This activity ensures they are connected to the greater good
4. They work together
5. And beyond their own narrow groups

The council can play a key role in promoting all of these things. For example, in Frome the IfF led council has supported: the annual street carnival, community clean-up campaigns, a Christmas meal for those otherwise on their own, massive expansion of allotments and intergenerational activities. This is Localism from the bottom up – not complex or expensive but strategic and targeted activity. It means hearing what people want, seeing where their energies lie and building on these. It has nothing to do with party politics or ego.

At a local level, how much money does it cost to set up an Independent party?

Here are two examples: IfF put up 17 candidates in 2011. Each of us put in £50 plus we had around £150 in donations. That's around £100 for each of the 10 new councillors. Liskeard put up 12 candidates in 2013. They each put in around £30 and with 10 elected that's around £36 for each new councillor. Costs are considerably reduced by working together as a group. In neither case does this calculation include costs of celebratory drinks, which I suspect roughly equal the declared elections costs. Costs to stand at district, County or MP levels would of course be greater – there is also a £500 deposit for MPs and £5,000 for MEPs which you lose if you get less than 2.5% of the turnout. My main point is that at a local level the cost is not great and in Frome we could have easily raised more from supporters as well. As a town or parish councillor you are not personally remunerated, though at District and County level you will be (see 'Who Gets Paid What' in Before We Begin', Chapter 4).

At a local level, how much time does being a councillor take?

Both Frome and Liskeard went public around three months before the elections (with a few weeks of plotting prior to this). In Frome we met every few weeks at first, more frequently nearer the election. All of us delivered leaflets and some of us did additional campaigning.

Since being elected, a few of us often put in between 10 and 20 hours a week, others have come closer to around one meeting every month. At any given time, an individual may do a lot or not much. Crucially, many of our meetings are light and entertaining – personally, I haven't laughed so much for years. By changing the culture we've reduced the stress. Greater activity seems to lead to greater engagement and achievement. After two years we'd got the right people in the right jobs and closer to the right structure so the need for councillor time was much reduced. Again, at higher levels time commitment would be greater. Apparently, over all, councillors spend an average of 23 hours a week. However, this includes those paid to attend meetings.

Is it worth it?

Only you can answer this question but at Open Liskeard's first public meeting the core group presented the crowd with three choices:

1. Do nothing
2. Encourage a few independent candidates
3. Form a group and go for the lot

It took about three seconds to choose option three, to a huge roar of approval from the floor.

Appendix 1 gives the profiles of the diverse group that makes up IfF. It is aimed to encourage anyone, along the lines of 'well if they can, so can I'. In Appendix 2 I describe some of the things that would definitely not have happened without us. They go way beyond those of a 'normal' parish council. I hope they will inspire you to keep reading and go for revolution.

As an aside, the more I have researched this guide, the more horrified I have become at the extent and degree of dysfunctional representation and the extent to which systems are not fit for purpose at the local levels of government. So many people I have talked to trump my worst examples of neglect and corruption. Most galling of all, though, is the missed opportunity. I believe the fragile possibilities presented through Localism not only can, but must, be grasped if we are to avoid significant social breakdown and damage that will take generations to recover from.

So, hopefully onwards, convinced of the need, inspired by the experiences of others and emboldened with a desire to do your bit? The next section of this guide covers what you need to do to build a functioning Independent Movement and get yourselves elected.

4. Before we Begin

IiF election poster

Frome is a market town of around 27,000 residents comprising about 11,000 households. It takes a pleasant half an hour to walk from one side to the other. Geographically, it is situated just to the south of Bath in the top right-hand corner of Somerset.

Frome has a history of both neglect and slightly bolshy independence. Originally it was a centre for the wool industry with power provided by the river Frome. This was replaced by iron mining and working, and later a specialism in printing. Almost all of these larger firms are now gone. Employment is now mainly provided by the mixed industrial estates on the edge of town and a plethora of new arts and design based small-scale companies within. On the outskirts of Frome the existing large 1970s housing estates, built as dormitories for workers in Bath and Bristol, are about to be added to in another large wave of house building.

Frome was made an Urban District Council in 1894 and remained so until its demotion to a town/parish in 1974 when significant land and buildings were handed over to Mendip, the new district council. The town council is the largest in the district with a budget of roughly £1m a year. politically, Liberal Democrat MP David Heath has been based in the town for 16 years and there has been strong Liberal Democrat representation at all levels. Recent town councils have been Liberal Democrat dominated with a Tory minority and a scattering of independents and Labour councillors.

In this guide I will also make special reference to Liskeard: a Cornish town of roughly 10,000 people. There had been no town elections in Liskeard for many years because of a lack of candidates. Hearing of Frome's 'democratic revolution', they sought our support and Independents for Frome attended an initial public meeting. Open Liskeard went on to dramatically take power in the town council elections as well as taking two county council seats. There are interesting lessons to be learned from the journeys taken by both towns. The key features of both Frome and Liskeard independents is that they are operating as a group of individuals, held together by a 'Way of Working', but not linked to any of the traditional political parties or the rules and structures within which they operate.

This guide focuses on the story of how the Frome group came together in 2011, took power and now work together for the benefit of the townspeople. There were 17 heads that poked above Frome's political parapet. Ten of them were elected. The two things they had in common was their lack of political experience and their desire for change. Their personal statements, culled from their own election addresses, can be found in found in Appendix 1.

United Kingdom structures of democracy.

Most people's understanding of the structures of democracy in the UK is not so good. So, here are the boring basics you need to know to in order to engage with the ideas that follow.

Q: Who represents you?
A: Somewhere between 3 and 12 people at various levels. (I know that's not very precise, but the system is both complex and irrational.)

In England, primarily in rural areas, you are represented by councillors at three tiers of local government: Town/parish, district and county. Then on top of that, a representative in the national Parliament (or House of Commons) and the European Parliament.

So, in Oakfield, Frome, I am democratically represented by, and can elect:

- Two town councillors for Oakfield Ward in Frome.
- One district councillor for Mendip District who represents Oakfield.
- One Somerset County councillor for Frome East.
- One Member of Parliament for the area of Somerton and Frome.
- Six Members of the European Parliament (MEPs) who represent South West England.

Each representative has their own area of responsibility, though there is sometimes an overlap.

In other parts of the country, there's just one (unitary) structure providing all the local services. These are in London boroughs, and some cities.

So my friend Tim in the city of Newcastle has his ward councillor for Wingrove, an MP and three members of the European Parliament who represent the North East.

Scotland and Wales have unitary councils and a layer of community councils. In Wales the community councils are roughly equivalent to parish councils in the way they operate. In Scotland they are only a consultative body and have no direct say in service delivery.

There are also a number of elected mayors (see below).

After many years of direct rule from the UK, Northern Ireland has its own parliament and 26 districts with elected representatives. These have significantly fewer powers than their equivalent bodies in the rest of the UK. It is intended that they will move to something closer to a Scottish/Welsh model by 2015.

Who does what?

There are roughly 9,000 English town/parish councils and Welsh community councils and they are responsible for local issues such as providing allotments, bus shelters, community centres, parks, play areas and play equipment, and grants to help local organisations. They are consulted on planning but don't make decisions. There is no difference in powers between town and parish councils. The Localism Act of 2011, along with its 'Power of General Competence', has greatly changed and potentially increased power at this level, but this is only slowly and erratically being used. I will look at the Localism Act in more detail in later chapters.

The 201 English districts cover services like: rubbish collection, recycling, Council Tax collection, housing and planning applications. They have the power to issue fixed penalty fines for things like litter, graffiti, fly posting and dog offences.

The 27 English county councils are responsible for services like education, transport, planning, fire and public safety, social care, libraries, waste management and trading standards.

So, in Frome, for example, if you report a weed problem in the road it should be to the Frome County Council. If it is on the pavement, it should go to the district Council. In reality there is probably much confusion: both of them have contracted their services to a commercial company and often no one deals with your weeds, unless perhaps it is the worker employed by the town council, acting out of desperation to get a problem solved. Many council websites do a good job of supporting people through the maze of responsibility, whilst others cause frustration and apathy, as it is often impossible to find who is responsible for what.

The services above are provided by 55 English, 32 Scottish, 22 Welsh and 26 Northern Irish Unitary Authorities along with 32 London and 36 metropolitan boroughs. In London and metropolitan areas some, like fire, police and public transport, are provided through 'joint authorities' (in London by the Greater London Authority). 'City' and 'borough' are titles of honour which do not affect the functions of a local authority.

In addition to all that, sixteen cities in England and Wales currently have directly elected mayors, with responsibility for some areas of policy and with the council acting in agreement or to veto their activity.

And who does what at national level? The elected parliaments of Scotland, Wales and Northern Ireland have their own members with varying degrees of decision making ability on issues including education, the environment, health and social issues. The British Parliament in Westminster (where the Scots, Welsh and Northern Irish also have MPs) covers the same issues for England and also big national issues like immigration, defence and nuclear energy for the entire United Kingdom.

Then there is the European Parliament, with its own elected members. What it does is way beyond the remit of this guide, but it's worth noting that its members represent the second largest democratic electorate in the world (after the Parliament of India).

To complete the picture (and your confusion), maybe I should mention the completely unelected and unrepresentative House of Lords and the Queen. She was also unelected, when last I looked, and in theory she is politically impartial and has limited powers.

The officers

These are the people whose work it is to support the elected representatives and carry through the policies they generate. Collectively, they are known as civil servants and they range from the assistant to the town clerk at parish level, right through to roughly 50 'permanent secretaries' who head up the government departments. The relationship between the democratically elected representatives and the civil servants is crucial. In theory, power lies with the elected representatives, but often they will be totally dependent on the service they get from the civil servants who can make things happen, or make sure they don't.

Who gets paid what?

Parish, town and community councillors give their time voluntarily, though they can vote to allocate themselves expenses.

district councillors are allocated around £3,000 per annum, more if they have leadership roles, plus expenses.

County councillors receive around £10,000, rising to around £30,000 for leaders, plus expenses – with considerable variation depending on the size of the organisation.

Salaries of British Parliamentary MPs will shortly be £74,000, plus expenses. Salaries rise with responsibility and there is very considerable opportunity for earning through lobbying, directorships and consultancy during or after holding their post.

MEPs are paid roughly £71,000, plus expenses.

Lords can claim £300 a day when at the House, plus other expenses. The Queen gets just over £36m (but I am not sure knowing that is helpful).

5. The Essentials

As before, this section relates primarily to my experiences of taking power at a town council level – but many ideas and lessons will apply elsewhere. I believe there are five essential ingredients that underpin from the 'Frome Model'. You can tweak them, decide in what order to add them to the mix, or bung them all in from the start. They are:

1. Work as a group
2. Agree your Ways of Working
3. Use a facilitator
4. Get all the help you can
5. Keep it light

Essential No 1: Work as a Group.

Aside from the pleasures of working with like-minded individuals engaged in the same struggles, there are four important practical reasons to work as a group.

1. You are probably up against the political party machine and/or a group of councillors who have been there for years. In either case, they are experienced operators who know how it all works. They will have systems in place to register voters; prepare and deliver leaflets; take less able voters to the polling booth on the day and so on. They may well have contacts in the press and will know what the press wants. They will also have some funds. Coming up against this machine as individuals is daunting, taking it on as a group can be inspiring, creative and possible.

> "I spent 15 mins (all I could cope with) reading through the nomination form. I like to think that I'm not completely stupid but it was fairly tough going. It feels as though… the current political structure is protecting itself from outsiders. This is the kind of thing an established party knows and would do for a candidate."
>
> *Councillor Toby Eliot*

2. As a group you can operate in a well planned and coordinated manner. Together you will have time to get things done in a way individuals would not.

3. On the ballot papers each party has its logo and name. Individuals have their name and 'Independent'. Historically, Independent councillors have often been people with extreme political ideology. So extreme they don't fit in any party or have been thrown out of one. A group of Independents working together needs to disassociate themselves from the maverick and nutter individuals (and be aware that they may well want to snuggle up to you). A logo and a clear name will distinguish you from the rest. To do this you will need to register as a party. At parish level (community council in Wales) you can do this as a 'minor party'. Registration as a minor party can also protect a group's name in Scotland. A minor party doesn't have to submit as much information when applying to register, or be subject to the same degree of financial controls, compared to a registered political party. As I write it costs £150 to register initially and £25 a year thereafter. Sadly, at higher levels than that, you do have to register as a 'political party' but it is probably worth it. All the details of how to do this can be found at the Electoral Commission's very clear website. Note that registration will take up to 20 working days.

4. After the election, the largest grouping gets to choose the Mayor and Leader of the Council, if you have one. This choice might be made by a group of parties in a formal coalition, or a formal group of individuals. Whoever is in control manages the agenda. And, as everyone knows, what's on the agenda is what gets discussed. Usually the makeup of committees is divided up based on proportions in the different parties/groups. The majority on committees choose the Chair. At higher levels than parish or town council there will be a Leader who selects a Cabinet. So, clearly, being the largest party and having a majority enables you to choose the Chairs including the Mayor. Assuming you are serious about real change, this positioning is crucial because, like it or not, a group of Independents has to start off by playing the game and grab as much influence as it can. In my opinion, if you are to change systems and really rock the boat, being organised early on is essential. Once the new shape is in place, there will be plenty of space for true independence and creative structural thinking.

> "A party… traditionally suggests a strict adherence to a firm set of ideas or ideology; whipping freethinkers into line to ensure consistency… when voting – an allegiance to a wider party beyond the locality and a closed shop, "if you are not a member of our party you can't stand and we won't listen to you." We have all seen the end results of such actions over the last few months. We subscribe to none of the above. We are a group of people from all walks of life and all ages who accept that we come together from different perspectives and experiences; we welcome debate and independence of thought; we actively encourage freedom of action and there is no party discipline.
>
> *Letter from Councillor Pippa Goldfinger to the local paper.*

Essential No. 2: Agree your ways of working together.

I asked Mel Usher, Convenor of the IfF group, who works all over the country with different councils, if he knew of a one that was well run by a group of Independents. After a long pause, the answer came back, "it always ends in tears". After we were elected, one of the Tories said "I give it until Christmas". So we set out to try and understand why dysfunction and acrimonious collapse is the norm. We came up with two answers:

1. Most groups of Independents come together around a single cause – usually a negative one. They are 'anti Tesco' or 'anti hospital closure' or 'pro the ring road'. Once in power, the cause is won or lost and 'other' issues come up. They now find they have different views on the 'other' issues and have no mechanism to work through these and make common cause again. Egos and personal power issues emerge. This has to be countered by identifying the common causes. It doesn't matter what political ideology each individual has (or doesn't have) as long as they are prepared to put the common good first and agree to work towards that ideal.

2. Secondly, there is a tendency to retreat to where we feel safe. In a new group of candidates, an individual will want to talk about and champion the causes and issues they feel strongly and/or know about. This focuses on differences rather than similarities. Just as above, the lesson is to deal with how to work together before what to work on. New political parties identify issues and policy first, rather than looking at the human and personal aspects, which are what we care about as individuals. There will be considerable pressure to define what you believe in and what you stand for. Resist the pressure to be too prescriptive or flounder on the rocks of irrelevant disagreement.

In my view there are two different but parallel areas to cover early on. These are:

1. The internal mechanisms of working as a group – I call these the '**Ways of Working**'.

2. And what you want the council to do after an election – I call this outward looking area '**The Principles**'. This includes both how you want the council to operate, and what you want it to achieve.

Ways of Working need to be broached right from the start. The principles can evolve a bit later. As I write, Open Liskeard's revolution is struggling in a period of internal strife and one of the key players reflects that this is because they focussed on principles at the expense of 'Ways of Working'.

Essential No 3: You can't do this alone – use facilitators, friends, experts, people with skills.

I would maintain that a facilitator is essential, preferably for the first public meeting, definitely for the candidate selection process and then for as long as it takes to settle as a group. By facilitator I mean using a neutral person who has skills in group work. In Frome we used a professional group facilitator, Neil, who gave us his time free and continues to do so. He introduced a number of simple techniques that led us to arrive at decisions in inclusive ways, with the process as important as the product. If you don't have access to someone with those skills, get a neutral person to run the relevant meetings and take time to plan activity carefully. Without a facilitator, one of the group is likely to become a de-facto leader, which can bring the potential for both competition and for leaving them to do all the work. Appendix 3 includes a case study of IfF facilitation and two of Neil's key techniques.

> "Neil's brainstorming stuff really helped to crystallize thoughts, and in a prompt manner."
>
> *Clare Tayler (Candidate)*

More help

I believe there is a thirst for change and people are prepared to support this. Out there somewhere are people dying to amaze you with their YouTube skills, show off the inner workings of Facebook and Twitter away endlessly. Embrace them as soon as you can. From the start it is necessary to create a movement for change in which the future councillors play just one of the many roles needed. These skilled people are crucial members of your movement. It is easy to select candidates and then watch the 'supporters' melt away, leaving the candidates to walk the streets in endless canvassing AND do all the work for the following four years. Celebrate the supporters' skills, include and consult them – especially if they are young.

Friends and relatives

Embrace them too. It's extraordinary how a team of five people delivers leaflets ten times faster than one person on their own. It may be the shared tales of carnivorous letter boxes; it may be the post delivery cake. You have no one in a shabby sports jacket driven by political idealism and zeal that will do this stuff for you – exploit your connections. Keep a list of helpers, supporters and sympathetic professionals – and treasure it. You'll want to call on them throughout your time in office and you'll certainly want to invite them to the parties.

Essential No. 4: Keep it light.

Independents for Frome is not a political party, but we do know how to party! From the start we have encouraged food and drink at meetings, we try not to go on too long and we positively encourage a degree of mirth. We are all volunteers and all busy people. Words like 'worthy', 'admirable', 'duty' and 'giving back' need to be banned at an early point. Also this is a brilliant opportunity to meet and get to know people you'd never normally go near. Difference is scary – especially for the English. But you will need to take a deep breath, embrace it and enjoy. As actor John Cleese said, "there is a tendency to confuse seriousness with solemnity." Serious causes can and must be approached with good humour, otherwise they're boring and can't compete with the Premier League and Grand Theft Auto. IfF's campaign meetings were never a chore, and our monthly meetings are keenly anticipated; our annual party/conferences have been a revelation…

> As far as local government meetings go, it's an unusual one. I am seated at a large wooden table in a low-beamed kitchen; it's late evening, the red wine is flowing liberally and a stranger to my left is enthusiastically relating an anecdote about loincloths. Now, for most people, the words 'local government' will conjure up torturously dull images of grey, fusty, middle-aged doctrinaires sat in drab council chambers, but I'm in Frome, Somerset:

> a town which has a group of councillors quite unlike any other. This is their 'unofficial' monthly meeting and the man talking about loincloths, Peter Macfadyen, is an elected councillor. He is describing the costume he wore to a recent parade in the town centre; an event that also involved the Mayor, some giant palm leaves and copious amounts of gold body paint.
>
> *From 'What a democratic revolution in a Somerset Town could teach our political class' The Independent Nov 2012.*

Essential No, 5: a good name.

83% of rock bands break up in the process of deciding their new name. I made that statistic up, but you get the drift. However, it is worth spending time on this. Independents for Frome has an acronym of IfF, which was incredibly useful as 'IfF not now when? ' 'no IfFs and buts…' 'IfF only…' But what were Independents for Bristol (IFB) thinking when they could have been Bristol Independents Group with BIG ideas? (Step forward Bath…). It is well worth some brainstorming and research with the woman in the street to check what chimes and doesn't clash with something else. Then see if the ideal name is available as a unique website address (URL). Similarly Facebook and Twitter, though you can usually get something close enough to your name to be usable if the ideal is not available.

So, our merry (see tip 4) group now know how they will work together, have gathered a vast band of skilled and willing supporters and are ready to launch their new name on the lethargic masses in an election campaign. Read on.

6. The First Public Meeting

Author talks to press

The big question is how do you move from that heady decision, made by a few people to enter politics, into a Barak Obama style mass movement? The most obvious start point seems to be a public meeting. That's what happened in Frome and Liskeard, and no doubt countless other places. Three months before the election feels about right – start earlier and you will run out of energy and risk peaking too early. For the launch event you don't need much, but below are some absolute essentials. Don't forget first impressions are vital:

1. **An accessible venue** booked well in advance. With a bar.

2. **Good and plentiful publicity** – leaflets, posters, emails to friends and acquaintances and so on. Make temporary Facebook and Twitter accounts if you haven't firmed up on a name (it only takes minutes). It's really important that you don't only get six people and a dog for this one.

3. **The press** – call the local press people and persuade them to come, with a photographer if possible. If they can't or won't, feed them with press releases. (Focus on personal stories, exciting, new, dangerous…)

4. **A plan.** This will be the moment many people join… or don't. Be clear who is going to do what. If you can get some well-known, rabble-rousing speaker to whip up the crowd for five minutes – great. BUT if you do this, make sure you know what they plan to say and are on your script not theirs. You could try asking someone like me who's covered part of the journey already. Be clear about what exactly you are going to ask of people. In Frome we already had some prospective candidates, so they spoke in order to encourage others. Our key aims were to get as many people on board as possible; pin them down to promises of specific support, and get more candidates.

5. **Have the basic information to hand**: When will candidates need to be declared? Roughly how much might it cost? Who is and is not eligible? What kind of support do you need? How many wards/seats are there? What is the current political make up of the council? Who are the current councillors? What have they done – or not done? But also leave space for ideas you haven't come up with – the more ownership and engagement, the more chance you won't end up on your own. All this will entail a bit of web research. The current town council website should give wards and councillors; the Election Maps website gives maps of wards and all other electoral divisions; and the excellent and indispensible Electoral Commission website is very clear on tricky rules on eligibility related to where you live, how long it must be since your prison sentence etc.

6. **A way to record who came and what they offered.** Sounds obvious, but make sure you get names, phone numbers and any special offers people can make. Collecting clearly written emails is essential – your campaign will be run through the email list. Supporters are key in so many ways and linking them in to this moment of creation with its special energy and excitement is really important. It's horribly easy for things to slip back to the core group, but actually people want to be engaged in all kinds of ways.

7. **Ask for money.** You may be surprised how much you will get even at this stage. Keep asking for money too – in Frome, the birthday party after two years raised £160.

8. **Did I mention the bar?**

The meeting.

Go for a short, exciting and upbeat meeting with a clear indication of what happens next. It also needs to be clear that you want to establish a large group of people with a range of roles, some of whom will be candidates. Don't let people think they are off the hook once candidates are selected.

Follow up very soon after the meeting with an email saying "thanks for coming and here's what we are doing next…". If you have reached the point of choosing candidates, let supporters know to maintain momentum. Also follow up with Facebook and Twitter – both of which can happen with pictures from the meeting itself. What you are looking for is both a warm glow from those who came and a feeling of having missed something really great from those who didn't.

From this point on a number of things will start to move together. Each group will decide its own priorities based on their own situation. But whatever the timing, there are essentially two areas to cover:

1. Who key people will be – including candidates
2. What else happens and when …. (better known as 'a plan').

In Frome, the initial concept of IfF came from a group that met in a pub. From this meeting a few other key individuals were identified and drawn in. This expanded group had some ideas on what they wanted to achieve and moved quite quickly to identify some initial candidates. Had the initial group continued to develop ideas, I believe it would have risked excluding key people who joined later. However, if the ideas aren't really formed at all, you risk choosing candidates with too wide a range of approaches, making working together impossible. What you are aiming for is diversity, held together by a common cause of interests and a rejection of party politics. Our initial group set out the framework of how to operate and a broad ethos, without restricting the ideas from new recruits. As with all of our ideas, there is no right and wrong way, but being aware of the risks of alienating supporters by setting ideas in stone too early is important.

The Flatpack Democracy Blog at **flatpackdemocracy.org** includes a number of press releases and notes from the initial meetings we held in Frome for further reference.

7. Choosing the Candidates

Pippa Goldfinger of IfF discusses politics on the Soap Box

From the initial meeting, by word of mouth, by arm-twisting and possibly by consciously targeting people you may want (women, youth, a wider class base), a list emerges. Ideally, there are more people wanting to stand than seats. This happened in Frome and so we asked each candidate – including those who had initiated IfF – to write half a page on why they wanted to stand. A group of those most active from the initial meeting, who didn't want to stand themselves, then selected from the list. This was a useful part of sharing the ownership/blame. A task of the selectors was to put together a group of individuals who could work together and had a good chance of taking power. That means not necessarily choosing the most experienced individuals, the best looking or the loudest voices. It is up to you to decide whether to go for positive discrimination in relation to gender, age or other criteria.

Personally, I would have liked to have seen more women candidates, either by making this known as we went public or by a positive bias in the selection process. If we are aiming for a less confrontational and more responsive local government, using most traditional male politicians as a template is a very poor place to start. Satish Kumar, editor of *Resurgence* magazine, has said: "We have one mouth and two ears and we should listen twice as much as we speak." In general women tend to listen better and F2M should be a guiding principle.

The initial group of people who formed IfF were primarily middle class professionals from a range of backgrounds (see Appendix 1). Our average age was around 45. After the election, only three IfF councillors were women (though six of the candidates were). All of us are white. This is not ideal in terms of representation but there are two things to say:

Firstly, it was ever thus. The National Census of Local Authority Councillors of 2010 showed that the average age was 60 (up from 55 in 1997). Two thirds were men, and 96% are white. Councillors are traditionally the shopkeepers and professionals with a certain amount of time and money to spare. This is still true, with the exception of career politicians who come in at local levels of politics. Their aim is climb the greasy pole as fast as possible to claim the prize of £65,000 (plus expenses) as a backbench MP.

Secondly, people new to towns often find themselves in organising roles and end up standing as councillors. There is evidence that this is because newcomers seek to build the networks that long-standing families and communities already have. So a group of largely middle class, older than average, mostly men is pretty much the norm. I say this not to defend the makeup of the group but to reflect that who we were was not exceptional in those terms.

However, once elected there are opportunities to redress some of the balance. As councillors you can personally seek new skills and experiences; you can bring in ways to consult that engage across the community and look to positively include areas previously left out. So, I believe it is best not to agonise too much about statistical representation – enthusiasm and desire for change are much more important.

> "Although criticised by some, I think sifting original applicants to get a good variety of ages, skills, interests etc. was worthwhile."
>
> *Clare Tayler (candidate)*

Who stands where?

Our default position was standing in the ward you lived in. If there were too many people in one ward, we drew lots. On reflection, it might have been better to have used the selection committee to do this job as most wards had three candidates, and careful selection could have engineered 'attractive IfF groups'. I also believe that, at a local level, councillors serve the whole area not just their ward, and there is no particular allegiance by voters to someone living in their ward.

However, there is potential for spending a lot of time trying to guess where it is best to stand and where not, usually based on who might stand against you. Much will depend on the system in a given town. For example, in Frome there are six wards with two or three people elected from each. In Liskeard there are three wards with six or seven elected from each, which means you can come seventh in Liskeard and still get in. In my view its best not to get too hung up on this and go for victory everywhere you stand! There were others who disagreed:

> "In my view, a failure was the policy of letting people stand where they wanted and then drawing lots. Entirely understandable with a group of independents but I am sure that we could have got one or two more candidates in if we could have used a bit of persuasion to match candidates and wards."
>
> *John Birkett–Smith (IfF candidate)*

What I am very clear about is that you should put up candidates for every seat. This is because you can't sell change to the public if they can see that at best you will be a minority with no chance of real power. You have just one chance to come from nowhere and, you can't change the system unless you control it. Linked to this, revolution is much more fun than polite protest from the 'back benches'! Also you might be surprised where you win, if there has been little choice for years, a new face might suddenly become attractive.

After choosing candidates and wards, it is essential to appoint an agent. This is the person who will look after the paperwork. They could be a candidate but if you can spread the load, do. You need someone to collect/download the 'nomination packs' and make sure all the papers are properly signed and returned by the right date. Do this early on to make sure there are no vital dates missed.

(In Frome we neglected to keep the three people who were not selected properly on board. This also applies to the candidates not elected. They could and probably should have been offered roles as critical friends. This would have given them a profile within the supporters, and potentially kept them engaged throughout and for the next election.

So, having got the group of candidates, the next chapter looks at how they should work together.

> The Flatpack Democracy Blog at **flatpackdemocracy.org** includes a number of press releases and notes from the initial meetings we held in Frome for further reference.

8. How to Operate as a Group

IfF councillors take a break during the 'party conference'

This chapter looks at three interconnected areas.

Firstly, I believe that, at all levels, for a group of individuals to operate for the common good and outside of a political party system, you will need to sign up to some kind of 'Way of Working'.

Secondly, if you are to change the systems of local government, you will need to set out how you will operate in office.

Thirdly, you will need to go some way towards describing how you will work with local people and what you hope to do in office. This means describing the relationship that you intend to build between you, the council and the people.

This is the key section of this guide, as it focuses on the essential difference between a collection of individuals and a group working together to achieve ambitious goals. It defines what we have tried to do differently in Frome. Compared to the rest of the guide, it is quite heavy going – but well worth the effort.

Way of Working (WoW).

As a group of people working together, and often under stress, it is essential that you devise and settle on your own 'Way of Working'. You do not have the comfort blanket of a party machine with preset rules and expectations. You will need to devise a way of working amongst yourselves that will lead to outcomes that reflect the beliefs and ethos of the whole group as well as possible.

In Frome, we devised our WoW early on in a session with all the candidates, facilitated by Neil, our professional external facilitator. In my view, the process of devising it is almost as important as the outcome. It will be an early opportunity to share ideas and start to build a group that is working in the same direction.

In preparing your WoW there is much experience to draw on from the Occupy Movement and other 'horizontal' and inclusive decision-making organisations. For example, a 'Community of Practice' is not a new concept, but a relatively new term. These are groups of people who share a concern or a passion for something they do. They learn how to do it better as they interact regularly. They might be a tribe learning to survive, a band of artists seeking new forms of expression, a group of engineers working on similar problems, or a group of individuals giving their time voluntarily to seek new ways to improve their local community.

The core elements of Communities of Practice are reflection and learning. I believe strongly that taking risks and making mistakes is positive, as long as we accept the mistakes and learn from them. In a fast changing world, we need to develop the confidence to take calculated risks, learn quickly and make adjustments. The current systems that most types of council operate on are the complete opposite. Their decision making processes remind me of a supertanker trying and failing to turn rapidly as it lumbers onto the rocks. Their default position is 'do what we did last year, and adjust for inflation'. Mel Usher (IfF convenor and council leader) advocates a 'Ready, Fire, Aim' philosophy. This is a short-hand way of saying that sometimes we spend so long aiming, we never actually fire. A further thought comes from the strap line of *STIR*, a new magazine writing about co-operative movements: 'Anger, Analysis, Action'. One of the IfF councillors, Graham Burgess, had this to say about the process of finding a Way of Working:

> "For the past 25 years I have attended summer camps in the UK and it is on this experience which I draw most heavily in my capacity as IfF councillor. These camps generally have a focus such as dance or singing, and the group is closed once everyone has arrived. One, in which I have a core role, puts its main focus on building a coherent community as fast as

possible. The core group of ten people meet each morning to share difficulties and joys, whether personal or organisational. The first thing we do is to try to learn all 120 names, through mixing people of the full range of ages and abilities. We facilitate spontaneity, community and trust through singing, cooking and playing together. It is amazing how quickly this can be done, and how exhilarating and fulfilling this can be for all concerned. It is my firm belief that contentment and happiness is more likely to occur where there is a sense of one's place within a community and where people feel able to participate in providing for themselves and their community in some way. In other words, the antidote to alienation is participation."

The IfF 'Ways of Working' documents are prefaced by this quote from Peit Hein, the Danish scientist, mathematician, inventor and poet: "The noble art of losing face may one day save the human race."

Admitting to mistakes is an anathema in current politics. The U-Turn is seen as a disaster; another legacy of Mrs Thatcher and her infamous "The lady is not for turning" speech. In real life, we constantly seek and take advice in order to adjust a position. As a politician, it is a constant challenge not to revert to the adversarial comedy of traditional council and parliamentary 'debate'. However, the way you behave is central to generating a different model with wide public appeal. For me, this underpins much of the ethos of a functional group of independents. We must not simply replicate the hierarchical structures of the past, dominated by Loud Men, with hierarchical structures of the future dominated by Nice People: fundamental change is required.

> "It's very disarming for your opponent when you are able to stand up and admit you got something wrong… these people thrive on argument, so by being honest you take their artillery away."
>
> *Mel Usher, IfF councillor*

Here are the main elements of the WoW we use. What they have done for IfF is provide an underlying ethos of trust and acceptance in the context of working for a common cause:

1. A willingness and ability to participate in rational debate leading to a conclusion.

2. Understanding the difference between constructive debate and personal attacks.

3. Avoidance of identifying ourselves so personally with a particular position that this in itself excludes constructive debate.

4. Preparedness to being swayed by the arguments of others and admitting mistakes.

5. Relative freedom from any overriding dogma or ideology which would preclude listening to the views of others.

6. Trust, confidence and optimism in other people's expertise and knowledge.

7. Confidence in the mechanisms and processes of decision-making that we establish, accepting that the decisions of the majority are paramount.

8. An acceptance that 'you win some, you lose some'; it's usually nothing personal and there's really no point in taking defeats to heart.

> "Democracy is the art of thinking independently together."
>
> *Alexander Meikljohn*

2. The Principles of how you will behave in office.

The Principles behind your WoW also need to extend into how you will work in relation to the public. Rather than reinventing the wheel, a key document you may want to adopt or adapt is the *Bell Principles of Independent Politics.* They are based on the ideas of Martin Bell, who was elected as an Independent MP on an anti-corruption ticket. The ideas were later adapted by the Independent Network, which aims to promote and support independent candidates and non-party politicians. While this document was formulated to apply to national government, many of the principles can be applied at all other levels. For example, all the independents who recently took power on the Isle of Wight signed up to the Bell Principles before campaigning. Gratifyingly, many of them overlap with Frome's Way of Working.

The Bell Principles cover both individuals and group behaviour, and also concepts of how the group sees democracy operating: 'Listening, consulting our communities constantly and innovatively'.

1. Abide wholeheartedly by the spirit and letter of the Seven Principles of Public Life set out by Lord Nolan in 1995: selflessness, integrity, objectivity, accountability, openness, honesty and leadership.

2. Be guided by considered evidence, our real world experience and expertise, our constituencies and our consciences.

3. Be free from the control of any political party, pressure group or whip.

4. Be non-discriminatory, ethical and committed to pluralism.

5. Make decisions transparently and openly at every stage and level of the political process, enabling people to see how decisions are made and the evidence on which they are based.

6. Listen: consult our communities constantly and innovatively.

7. Treat political opponents with courtesy and respect, challenging them when we believe they are wrong, and agreeing with them when we believe they are right.

8. Resist abuses of power and patronage, and promote democracy at every level.

9. Work with other elected independents as a group, with a chosen spokesperson.

10. Claim expenses, salaries and compensation openly so the public can judge the value for money of our activities.

It may be helpful not to restrict early meetings just to the candidates but to invite key supporters as well. To build skills and keep things informative, you may also want to invite short upbeat inputs from other outsiders. For example, in Frome we had presentations from a marketing expert, and someone with inside information on the Localism Act. What you are attempting in this process is to cover key elements of information and campaign planning that political parties have taken decades to do – in a few weeks. And that's fine, providing you allow for constant evolution, and acknowledge and learn from your mistakes.

As a variant on the theme, below are the key principles set out by a group of existing councillors in Northampton County Council who chose to form an Independent Group in 2009. Note that by becoming a formal group in this way they had rights to proportional representation on committees (as described in Chapter 5, Essentials, No. 1, point 4).

Independence: we are not a political party, and we will follow no party/group whip, nor impose on our group members any actions other than to respect our core values and principles. We will remain individual independent voices in council.

Equality: we believe that all are born and remain equal and all should have equal access to the same life opportunities and experiences; we abhor racism and intolerance and fight the injustices they bring. We will work together to achieve equality of opportunity for all citizens of Northampton and to all users of council services.

Honesty: we believe that politics, local and national has become riven with self interest and party manipulation and we will inform the citizens of the town through our actions and through council the true position of our town and council and let the people make their own judgements.

Truth: likewise, we believe that the public must always be told the truth, even when it is not pleasant for them to hear, we will therefore be open and truthful in all our dealings.

Local Pride: we believe in civic pride and we are proud of our heritage and at ease with our future. We want only what is best for our town. Therefore we will work constructively with other members and groups on council where we feel they have the best interests of the town at heart.

> "It is important that people understand that we are independents; of thought and of one another. We can subscribe to some broad principles but each one of us will make up his/her own mind on individual matters. So don't expect over refined statements of intent, don't look for buttoned up party discipline but do expect vigorous debate and the frequent use of the words, 'why?', and crucially, 'if'."
>
> *Mel Usher, IfF councillor, from a pre-election letter to the local paper*

3. Tell others HOW you will work with the people and WHAT will you do once you are in office.

For most people it seems to be too much of a challenge to envisage a group of individuals making coherent decisions without the familiar model of a manifesto and national policy guidelines. This is odd given that we do it all the time outside of politics, but for a new group of independents, creating that confidence is a huge challenge.

During the campaign and immediately after the election, the accusation that "you're secretly a party" is likely to be a key issue, especially at higher levels. This happened to us to a certain extent in Frome, and also in Liskeard, but even more so for the Bristol Independents and the Island Independents of the Isle of Wight (IoW). The follow up statement was generally "And if you are a party, what do you believe in?" In Frome, we produced broad direction on key issues on which there was group agreement. On the IoW they went much further, producing a comprehensive statement of principles and processes in their *Framework for Change* (a document well worth reading).

There is a tricky balance to be struck here. In reality, until you are in power, it's not possible to know exactly what policy and strategy will be. In Frome, early activity around leaflets, the website and other media quickly focussed attention on a key issue: What do we stand for? As an 'anti-party party', there was no traditional methodology for defining this. As IfF emerged, this was the key point picked on by mainstream party members in letters to the papers: "Why would you vote for something that doesn't know what it believes in?" 'The parties, on the other hand, hide behind a national manifesto: their local candidates tell you nothing except "I am Tory/LibDem/Labour/Green/UKIP..." This might have some credibility, except that a) national policy has little if any local relevance and b) once elected, promises are systematically broken.

However, it is essential to start the work of defining what you will do as a group of independents: not only to provide confidence around what actions you will take in power and what makes you different, but also because if/when you take power, you will have at least a skeleton outline of agreed proposals.

To better understand the two key areas I believe are essential, here are examples from the journey from initial discussions to final campaign material from Frome and Liskeard.

Firstly, how will a council run by independents work with the people?

Many groups wishing to change their local council do so because of actual and perceived problems with the current system and councillors. In setting out a Way of Working, you are likely to have started to focus on this. For example, you may want to form a group that will listen and respect views. This is already radically different from many parties, and from the way many local councils work: so tell people about it.

Open Liskeard used this approach as the core of their early appeal to voters. All the issues below (except the last) focus on discontent with the previous administration and what they will change in relation to how they will operate when in power. Their publicity leaflet on the right explains it all.

Open Liskeard
OUR TOWN. OUR FUTURE. OUR SAY

Open Liskeard - what we stand for

We want the Town Council to work effectively with the people of Liskeard to regenerate a vibrant and prosperous community that feels good about itself

To help make this happen we will be:-

Open to being judged by the electors of Liskeard through the ballot box

Open in the way we work with you and local organisations through public consultations and meetings

Open to change and new ideas in order to improve Liskeard

Open about when and how decisions are made through well-publicised meetings, with clear agendas and feedback

Open about what we have done, through published progress reports

Open to criticism when we have got things wrong – we will own up to our mistakes

Open about how we spend your money

Open for business – encouraging the growth of employment and shopping in the town

As independent candidates with individual views we will work together in the common cause of improving Liskeard

Frome's initial ten principles – put together on the back of an envelope in a cafe discussion – include four which cover similar territory:

1. Local people making local decisions in the local interest through non-party councillors that listen and act on what they hear.

2. Encouraging greater public involvement and consultation to ensure transparent local government, with no closed-door committees.

3. Rethinking the role of the council in relation to youth, arts, education, employment and the voluntary sector. Acting as a hub, facilitating all sectors to work together in the interests of Frome.

4. An end to corrosive traditional party politics which serve no purpose at a local level.

As before, these were adjusted and refined in a facilitated process that included candidates and supporters. I believe this is essential in defining the ethos of inclusivity and openness. If there is no scope for change and addition by newcomers, or as the project progresses, it will exclude potential engagement and reduce the possibility of exploring new ideas. Frome's six final principles emerged in this way and were adopted for campaigning and action once we were elected:

1. **Independence**. Traditional party politics are corrosive and serve no purpose at a local level. IfF councillors will be non-party and free to make decisions on behalf of the community without policy imposed from outside, nor with the requirement to vote as a block.

2. **Integrity**. We intend to introduce as much transparency and openness into the system as possible; limiting private meetings, providing easy access to minutes and decision making, and improving public involvement and consultation.

3. **A 'Can Do' approach**. The council can, and should, be the positive hub that helps to ensure the joint success of the private, public and voluntary sectors of Frome, sometimes thinking the 'unthinkable' to produce 'the supposedly undoable'.

4. **A new Sustainable way of working**. We want to rethink the role of the council to youth, arts, the elderly, education, employment and the voluntary sector whilst lobbying assertively for more resources for the town.

5. **Fairness**. A belief in fairness and compassion founded on a respect for local democracy producing a society run for all.

6. **Cleaner and Greener.** Developing creative alliances to make Frome a cleaner and greener place to live.

What I have described so far is essentially 'how' the group will operate. This may not satisfy the need of the electorate to know what will actually be done. They expect their candidates to say what they will do. The fact that this is usually a set of promises that are not kept is irrelevant. While I believe the focus should be firmly on who you are and how you will work, some compromise is necessary towards saying what you will do if elected.

The key things to develop and focus on are areas on which you agree. In Frome we identified broad headings – Community, Development (as in buildings), Environment, Arts, Business etc and for each, drew up key things we'd like to do. We then narrowed this down to one or two key actions in each area that we all agreed on.

For example, on the Environment we brainstormed a huge list, and then prioritised it to agreed areas including: promote a cleaner/greener Frome; plant more trees on public land; liaise with community groups; expand the provision of allotments, etc Some are general, some specific, some huge and some small – the point is that in the process of working together to develop clear, simple ideas, we found key common areas and non-divisive statements.

For each area, we then evolved an overarching statement and some specific things we'd do:

1. Revitalise local democracy by looking at alternative ways of engagement, consultation and decision making.
2. Examine the effectiveness and role of the council itself.
3. Provide an articulate, democratic and evidence-based voice for Frome.
4. Make sustainability a central plank of what we do and say.
5. Make best use of provisions in the new Localism Bill.

There is nothing especially radical in these statements or the methodology. But the sad truth is that at a parish or town level, this is rarely done at all. Candidates are elected on their national manifestos, and local strategy tends to be based on 'what we did last year'. The process I have described demands engagement and thought about local issues, and I believe that is attractive to voters. At city, district and county level, with large budgets and responsibilities for areas such as health and education, the group must have much clearer priorities and developed strategies. The key is to find common areas of agreement amongst the group and focus on these.

In Frome's campaign leaflets, the five statements became based around 'What do we stand for?'

1. Independence of thought
2. Integrity transparency and openness
3. Respect for local democracy
4. A society run by all
5. A cleaner and greener Frome

For each area, we spelt out specifics, for example: "Every year over the next four years we will focus on one specific group, (for example youth or the elderly), analyse the services provided for that group, survey individuals about provision, identify issues and produce tangible changes with other agencies."

I believe this represents a workable way to meet the need for specifics and an opportunity to explain a really new approach, without selling out to a manifesto of promises which voters do not respect (with good cause). It also forces the group to really engage and think about issues in their community that they might not usually consider.

So, forming the group and developing Ways of Working is, I believe, the first essential for success the electoral campaign. The principles of how you will relate to the public and what you would do given power will develop as you work together.

This quite detailed chapter also establishes how different IfF's ambition was and is. At this level of politics, getting elected is mostly about being persuaded to stand, doing virtually nothing to get elected and then muddling along for four years. We set out to see if things could be done differently.

Having developed the group and its ethos, and defined how you will behave in office, there comes the challenge of getting elected. This is the subject of the next two chapters, which cover specific guidance on how to do this.

9. Preparing a Campaign

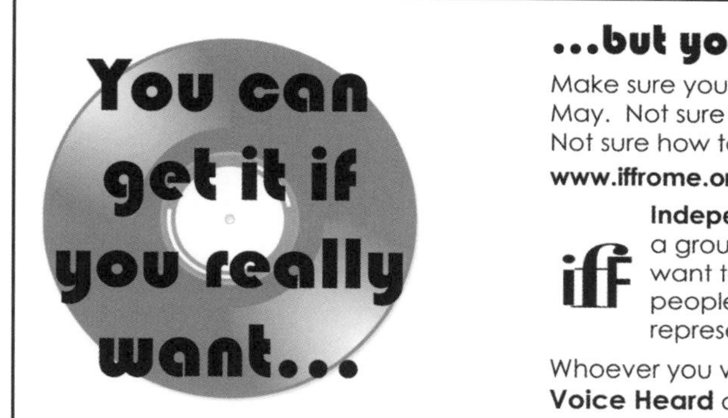

Leaflet that accompanied the flashmob choir at Sainsbury's

This chapter (and the following one which deals specifically with the media) aim to bring together ideas that will guide a group of independents towards a successful election campaign. As before, they are based on my experiences from Frome (a market town with roughly 27,000 people) and geared mainly towards parish/town levels – though hopefully the principles can be applied more widely.

A timetable.

Early on it is crucial that everyone knows when the election is, and when you must be registered as candidates. Work back from this to create a chart, making clear when tasks need to start. Some projects may have a long lead in time – for example creating a leaflet, or making advertisement boards to stick in gardens. Postal vote forms are sent out about a week before the election, so make sure your leafleting takes this into account. In a recent Frome by-election, 50% of votes were postal. Note that if you ask to postal vote once, you will be sent that option from then on – so numbers will probably grow. I suspect most people do their postal voting almost as soon as the ballot paper arrives, which means that early campaigning is essential to catch this important group of voters.

The last day to register as a voter is 11 working days before the election. This is the same timing as registering for a postal vote. Postal votes are a very important source of new voters especially amongst your family and friends' children, who may be away from home. Local elections are usually held in university term time, and national elections always are. An increasing number of people register for postal votes – apparently around one in five. More than two in three of those with a postal vote returned it, in contrast to less than one quarter of those required to vote in person. So you need to get those postal voters organised. Conversely, if your electoral area includes students, you don't want them to have registered for postal votes at home but to register at the university.

There are rules about what you can and cannot say to encourage postal voting and they focus on ensuring that the postal voter really is making the decision – see the Electoral Commission website.

Recommended Action Groups.

1. Admin/Nominations Group

An admin group and someone looking after nominations are crucial roles. If you can find someone reliable who's done it before, grab them as your agent. By definition, the election agent is the person legally responsible for the conduct of a candidate's political campaign, and the person to whom election material is sent by those running the election. At parish level, most candidates are their own agent. Whether formally your agent or not, having one person who is the central point for electoral information is a huge help. This person will need to put aside all bedtime reading in favour of 'Guidance for Candidates and Agents' from the Electoral Commissions website. There are separate sections of guidance for independents standing alone and within parties. Early on, you must check that all your candidates are eligible for election. The criteria are clearly laid out in the Guidance notes. For example – candidates need to be over 18, and can be a Commonwealth or EU citizen as well as British. They need to have lived in the electoral area for 12 months, not be bankrupt and have not served a long prison sentence in the last five years.

I definitely recommend the creation of a minor party if you are standing as a group in a parish. This requires much less paper work than a full political party, although currently the registration cost is £150 in either case. (All the details of how to do this are on the Electoral Commission website under 'guidance on registering and maintaining a party'). Your own Electoral Officer will publish a Notice of Election with crucial dates on websites and at council offices, including a final date for nomination and when forms need to be completed and presented. Befriend your local Electoral Officer as early as possible and they will hold your hand through the various forms required. It's not really that complex, but one mistake can mean you aren't in the mix.

The admin group/agent must also keep an eye on the rules and make sure the group's activity is complying with these. The guidance notes include 'campaigning dos and don'ts' and various rules. Most of these are pretty obvious, such as not paying canvassers, bribing, threatening by force etc. There may be local rules in place about where you can and cannot campaign – especially if you are on property owned by the council. Common sense seems to work pretty well, but there are plenty of people whose lives are dedicated to finding the small print you contravene. In Frome, we were handing out leaflets on what turned out to be council owned land, and were charged £25 for this after a political rival informed the council. As I am writing this a new Lobbying (or 'gagging') Bill and the Government's Anti-social Behaviour, Crime and Policing Bill legislation has just been passed by parliament – this allows councils to ban a range of activities which may include more creative campaigning and lobbying.

2. Accounts

You will need to keep accounts, to be presented within 28 days of the election. Again, the guidance notes are clear and include templates. The rules may change, so check the Electoral Commission website. Keep receipts for anything over £10. At present there is a maximum spend of £600, plus 5p per person on the electoral roll for your ward/election area, per candidate. If you are working as an official group, this is reduced by a third to reflect shared costs. So, for a group with 10 candidates and around 2,000 voters per ward, the total limit would be £4,667. This is around five times what we spent in Frome. At higher levels, there are more voters so the limit is higher. The whole ethos of *Flatpack Democracy* rests on community support, so I'd suggest that if you need to spend anywhere near the legal limits there is something wrong: you need to beef up your grassroots support and word-of-mouth networks, which are free, hugely effective and have the happy side-effect of empowering and including your supporters.

3. Coordination Group

The coordination group will be required to 'hold the centre'. Hopefully your group has a good mix of people and skills, from those with lots of ideas who can't actually do anything, through to quiet efficient ones who do everything but have no ideas! If it doesn't, then identify the gaps early on and enlist volunteers from the wider support group. Our coordination group organised four meetings every two weeks from the start of March to elections in early May. They organised public events such as leaflet handouts. They were also the focal point for decision making between meetings, and acted as a collective 'spokesperson'. Since then, Dropbox and Google Drive have become much more commonly used, making life infinitely easier, and potentially doing away with long email streams crossing and re-crossing with each other. You may need to bring everyone up to date on these, along with the wonders of Doodle to schedule meetings. If anyone isn't up to speed with the technology, you either need to accept that they will play a lesser role, or find other ways to include them.

4. Other Groups

I strongly recommend as flat a structure as possible, with different autonomous groups tasked and empowered to do their bit. As well as admin/nominations, the groups we had in Frome were Wacky Ideas, Leaflets, Display Boards, Social Media, Traditional Media, and Coordination. There were between one and five people in each group. Looking back, we should have involved more non-candidates and helpers in these groups.

Running the campaign.

We put up 17 candidates for 17 seats across all six wards. At the risk of stating the obvious, campaigning is selling yourself – both as a group and as individuals. Basic marketing rules apply here, just as they would if you were selling a new product.

Who is your market?

Some interesting facts culled from the Electoral Commission report on the 2013 Local Elections showed that only somewhere between one third and two thirds of registered voters actually voted. The remainder were largely 'too busy, forgot or were away'. These figures vary with age – 75% of those under 35 didn't vote in the last national election and in general older people are much more likely to vote – put down largely to 'civic duty'. Nearly one in five voters in my district of Mendip is over 70.

If you want to drill down into detail for your area, Googling 'voting patterns for X' brings up copious reports, but I suspect the overall message in terms of target is the same: the majority of people don't vote and those that do are likely to be elderly. I suspect that without a good reason to do otherwise, most people do what they always did: the British don't seem to do change very well. Especially at local levels, voting along purely party lines does not seem as prevalent as in higher levels of election. So recognisable candidates, and a good campaign based on local issues, have a great chance of breaking the mould. That said, and given that your group of independents represents change, I suspect a key market will be new and younger voters.

Once you have determined (or guessed) who the key people you want to target are, you need to devise a strategy to reach them.

So what is the strategy?

Focus on the easiest to convince first – and if there is time, try for some of the harder ones. Key points are:

1. Increase the number of voters – new voters are less likely to be set in their ways. By far the best way to do this is by standing in every seat. People who may not have had the opportunity to vote for years suddenly can. 75% more people cast votes in Frome than in 2007 mainly because we stood everywhere, compared to the district as a whole, where 46 out of 88 parishes had no election.

   Less effective – but valuable in other ways – is a voter registration campaign (see below). Keep in mind that the difference between success and failure may be very very few votes.

2. Spend time developing clear, simple, relevant messages. What's your 'Unique Selling Point': why are you different? Test this with supporters and relatives to see if what they hear is what you think you are saying.

3. Be different. The press are as bored of the usual non-event elections as the voters. You may lack the machinery of party public relations offices and their contacts with the local press, but you can offer new and newsworthy moments.

How to get the message out.

In Chapter 4 I covered creating the message – this section looks at how to ensure as many people as possible receive it. In Frome, based on the need to be different, the first campaign group we set up was the Wacky Ideas Group.

This group came up with all sorts of weird and wonderful campaigning ideas. As expected, there were some good really good ones and some that were completely off the wall. The supermarket flash-mob choir struck me as totally unworkable when I first heard it but was actually a huge success and led to regional TV coverage. It involved around 70 people in a local supermarket bursting into song – "You Can Get it IfF You Really Want..." at a prearranged signal. The whole event was so short that security (who were generally amused anyway) had no time to act, and the singers then dispersed.

The flash-mob event was followed up with a press release "…Shoppers and staff at Sainsbury's were taken by surprise when over 70 members of the public burst into song on a busy Friday evening, last week. The flash-mob was organised by IfF (Independents for Frome) who are standing as candidates in the forthcoming town council elections…"

> "I remember that at some point, wisely, we decided to NOT do some wacky stuff as we realised that if we pushed it too far people wouldn't take us seriously – not doing some things was important."
>
> *Pippa Goldfinger, IfF councillor*

The flash-mob choir aimed to raise our profile, but was also linked to a **Voter Registration Campaign**. This allows three things:

1. Having a reason to stop people and to chat to them

2. An increasing turnout with new voters. Our thinking was that the parties would get the core of voters who always voted for them. So to increase our share of the vote, we would need to bring in more voters, especially the traditionally disinterested and younger voters.

3. Getting around the 'balance issue'. For six weeks before an election there is a period of 'purdah'. This isn't legally enforced, but it means that currently elected councillors shouldn't use their position to support their campaign and that the press is likely to look for 'balance'. Increasing voter registration is generally seen as a good thing and not linked to a party.

We asked the parties if they would join us in the Voter Registration Campaign. Labour said they "would be pleased to support this initiative"; the LibDems said "we will be following our own arrangements on this type of election supporting issue. So you can progress with whatever you want to do without worrying about our involvement" and the Tories verbally said they had nothing against it. The local press were happy to support the registration with more coverage than they would give to just us. So we linked the flash-mob choir and some other street events to this element of the campaign. The main line was "We don't care who you vote for – just vote!" However, the fliers referenced IfF's website as the most effective way to register through a link, and it got our faces out and about. None of the parties had Facebook pages linked to the local election, and actually none did anything to increase registration.

Satisfyingly, and proving yet again that interest can be generated in local politics, we increased turnout by 75%.

A call to vote!

Throughout North Africa people are protesting, in part because they want working democracy and the right to a vote which counts. Not many generations ago women in Britain equally struggled for that right. Yet – especially in local elections – only around a third of people entitled to vote bother to do so. In seven weeks, elections for councillors for Frome town council take place (alongside Mendip and a referendum on the way we vote).

The three political parties and group of independents are all agreed that a higher turnout would be good for Frome. Over the next few years there will be many important decisions to be made in the town, and the new Localism Bill is set to ensure local views are really heard. The greater the degree of public engagement, the better chance there is that Frome will end up what the majority of its citizens want!

If you aren't yet registered, or need a postal or proxy vote, then it really needs to be done by April 1st.

Text from an IfF leaflet

Getting out there.

1.On the street

Leading up to the elections we regularly had a spot in the town centre to hand out leaflets and talk to people – one of the advantages of having a big group is that we could match the party machine and their dwindling band of volunteers in this way. We learnt that voter registration was not the only barrier to participation. Most people didn't know their ward and there was huge confusion between town, district and county representation. To help, we provided information on where polling stations were, how the wards were laid out and how the local elections worked. In Frome there was always more than one councillor to elect per ward. Often the parties had only one candidate in a ward, so accepting that many people will stick to their party with their first vote, encouraging them to use their other votes for us for us was crucial.

> "The real selling point in the early days (months before the election) was the focus not on securing victory but debunking the process. It's complicated voting at a local election and so unlike any other election that we vote in. We really had to push 'You have two or three votes'."
>
> *Toby Eliot, IfF councillor*

On the street there were broadly four groups of people:

1. Openly hostile – always be polite but waste as little time on them as possible.
2. People who hesitate and glance. Make sure the message on the stall, your leaflet and in your patter is instantly clear to draw them into conversation.
3. People show clear interest. Make sure you have a good reason for them to sign up and commit. Take time.
4. Obvious supporters. Get them to commit to doing something for the campaign. Counterintuitively, don't spend too much time talking to this group: they already support you. You need to focus on groups 2 and 3.

2. Leaflets and door knocking

Leaflets are generally thought to be essential. After the successful Liskeard campaign they said: "We managed the bread and butter tasks of election communication – a leaflet through every door before the postal votes were sent out and candidates knocking on as many doors as possible. Many people told us that they had put in postal votes for us on the basis of our leaflet. In the most hotly contested ward, the people who had done significantly more canvassing got significantly more votes."

Remember, the process of agreeing and distilling ideas and of campaign activity is as important as the actual product. Liskeard again: "The stall in the town centre, the leafleting of train commuters and the huge scale projection of images on a town centre wall were fun, and helped create a sense that something different was happening."

Top tips for an effective leaflet:

1. Keep it simple.
2. Seek expertise in design.
3. Be positive.
4. Black and white is good – the parties have colours, and black and white is cheap.
5. Ask for help and contact details whenever possible.
6. Guide the voter: explain the system. If there is more than one person elected in a ward, it is crucial that voters use all their votes.

My admiration for posties increased greatly after sustaining a cut knuckle from a savage attack by a Nunney Road letterbox. I was constantly trying to work out how best to hold open the flap, feed in the leaflet, not drop other leaflets, and avoid the razor sharp edge of the spring loaded bit.

Why stop at leaflets? A few moments on the web will lead you to personalised beermats, visiting cards, car stickers, T shirts etc. Some of it surprisingly cheap, and some is free (Vistaprint cards for example). It's probably counter-productive to spend a vast amount of time and money on this stuff, but it can quickly show that you exist, are serious and are wittier than what came before.

Everything you produce, including websites, must have what is called an 'imprint' on it. That is the name and address of the printer, promoter and anyone who the work is on behalf of. For example 'Printed and promoted by J Blake of 32 Acacia Avenue, W1 1ZZ, for and on behalf of Independents for Frome'. We failed to do this on our boards as they were hand painted and an observant rival told the Electoral Commission, who duly told us to correct or remove them. It took a while sticking on little labels or writing the bumph in biro, but it also built up anti-pedant energy which was useful in campaigning.

In Frome we delivered three A4 black and white leaflets over a 6 week period. The first set out:

- Who we are.
- What we stand for.
- How you can help.

It had some broad statements based on 'IfF only…', such as 'IfF only… we could have a greener cleaner Frome'. Leading to 'IfF you want change… vote for it'. The reverse was a whole page poster.

The second leaflet gave headlines of the Principles and Policies (how we'd operate as a council and what we'd do). The reverse was a full page of all the candidates giving a photo and single upbeat paragraph on each of our beliefs. This is an important opportunity to show a range of age, gender, background and skills (if you have these!). We made sure that this was delivered before postal voting had started.

Finally, on the eve of the polls we circulated details of polling arrangements, and the names of candidates in each ward (along with top line, large print, headlines encouraging change – 'IfF you do what you always did, you'll get what you got'.

> As always with a bunch of independents, not everyone agreed: "I didn't like final leaflet (the candidate's name with an X beside it): I felt it was too traditional, and not in keeping with avoiding that sort of thing."
>
> *Clare Tayler, IfF candidate*

We also produced a small 'Sorry you were out' slip to go with door knocking.

It could be argued that this was massive overkill: most of the political parties managed only one leaflet drop. Liskeard may be more the norm: "...there was little other town council election activity from the other candidates, so getting the basics right had a disproportionate effect." The number of votes cast in most town/parish elections is often extraordinarily small, so only a few votes make the difference. One of the IfF councillors was elected by a single vote. To illustrate this, the following table shows voting in a typical ward in Frome which elected three councillors from six candidates:

Votes	Difference	
557	+27	Elected
530	+12	Elected
518	0	Elected
502	-16	Not elected
496	- 22	Not elected
492	-26	Not elected

Where candidates, or well-informed supporters, are delivering leaflets, this can be combined with door knocking. I was against this on the grounds of being a coward, but am now convinced it's an essential tool not only to persuade voters to vote independent, but also to vote at all. An alarming number of people either didn't know or didn't care. They had no idea the date of the election, what it was for or even where the polling station was. In only one case was I met with rudeness – and this was essentially: "I've already made my mind up so don't waste your time."

Timing is important. Avoid key TV moments, meal times and waking small children. Cause them to miss the vital goal, or wake the baby, and you are off to a bad start. Remember to ask about all those who can vote in the house: just because he's set on voting Tory, it doesn't mean she or the children are. Also, there may be one only party candidate and more votes going spare – don't let them be wasted.

> "It's great that so many people are taking letter-box draught-proofing so seriously, but just how do Royal Mail protect the hands of their postal delivery staff? Also how do they protect them against dogs? Several of my leaflets disappeared straight into the mouths of waiting pooches, and I managed to liberate one dog from its garden and had to retrieve it from the street before I could continue my round."
>
> *Tricia Golinski, iFf councillor*

Each official party is entitled to one copy of the full electoral register, available from the Electoral Officer. This will be on paper or electronic. You can also access edited versions on line but they are essentially for junk mail, and don't give absolutely up to date information. The official pre-election version is really helpful to see how many voters are at each address, including where people are voting by proxy or post. Whether you will have time for this level of analysis is questionable – we didn't analyse, we delivered to every house. The register is also useful to organise delivery as you can allocate streets easily (especially with the electronic version). In accepting the copy you agree to rules on its use which come with it – there is a £5,000 fine for breaking these.

> "What worked for me during the campaigning will not work for everyone as it is down to individual style and personality, but I found the best way to get my message over was to engage the electorate in non-threatening places and locations, where it was easy for them to walk away if they so wish. The people that wanted to be engaged hung around to hear my pitch. Outside of Tesco Express was ideal and I feel very effective, much more so than buttonholing people on their doorstep, which can create resentment rather than interest. For all the reach that Twitter and Facebook can offer, you still cannot beat the face to face pitch, particularly if you have a new message to deliver. So I guess I am saying that you have to put in the hard yardage as well as all the new sexy stuff."
>
> *Nick White – IfF councillor.*

3. Signs

Signs in people's gardens and other prominent places can really raise the game. They are potentially high input in terms of money and time, and can be vandalised, but are a great opportunity to let people know something is afoot. With the aim of piquing peoples interest, we went for an untraditional approach, with signs in key places in the shape of speech and thought bubbles with enigmatic comments: "IfF not now when", "IfF only..." and "B..... IfF" (which was possibly too obscure even for us). We also produced standard A4 signs with candidate's names on. A significant number is important to give the clear message that this is real movement – too few may be worse than none at all. Signs need to comply with any planning legislation, for example not obscuring road junctions. The opposition is likely to be surprisingly vigilant in reminding planning officers of their duty. Signs also have to come down within two weeks of the election.

> "I liked 'non-shiny' handmade look of boards."
>
> *Claire Taylor, IfF candidate*

10. The Media – a Strategy

Press photo of councillors replacing asphalt with heritage paving slabs

A media strategy is vital to success. It is the nuts, bolts and Allen keys that hold the campaign together and make it visible and vibrant.

My advice would be, if at all possible and as early in the process as possible, to get on board a person who understands how these things work. You'll need them to donate their time to running the press side of the campaign and hopefully bringing others up to speed with the techniques that matter. Obviously, they must be sympathetic to your cause and be prepared to work in a way, outlined below, that is different from the usual negatively biased, political media circus. If possible, also get a person or group who will record events and incidents on film or in photographs. Pictures are very useful for the website, press releases and leaflets.

Overall a media strategy needs to do two things:

1. Ensure that who you are and what you do is broadcast as widely as possible.

2. And allow the engagement of potential voters in the movement and the wider political process.

Using the various media outlets, it is possible to provide the message of optimism and change from the old system that I believe voters want to hear.

As an underlying theme, it helps if your strategy is aimed at increasing overall interest in local engagement with decision making. Sharing information on the work of local groups, talking about local issues and linking these to regional and national stories is always good. This gets you out of the ghetto of being 'just another party' and expands your reach out of their negativity.

I have divided the media into TWO groups, 'old' and 'new', though inevitably they overlap.

Old media:

Newspaper and magazine coverage, letters to the press, TV, radio etc.

It is essential to recognise that you can feed stories to the above media outlets, but ultimately you don't control what is used or when.

The key with old media is not to get drawn into anything that looks like traditional politics. Clearly, if you have any contacts with editors of local papers or local TV and radio, use them ruthlessly. Newspapers and TV have an annoying tendency to look for what they consider to be balance. (Witness how climate change deniers are wheeled out in any discussion despite the fact that 99% of scientists accept it as fact. This also provides a salutary lesson as to the power of the media: 15% of the British population now doubts climate change compared to 5% five years ago, according to the Observer, 22nd September 2013).

What is newsworthy?

Always remember that editors are looking for stories and news which is different, funny or controversial. News that is local has plenty of personal and human interest, drama and emotion, which is good. It needs to be new and important to a significant number of people. Humour and pictures are really helpful. A good measure of a story is if it survives a 'so what' test? In other words, would a neutral reader finish feeling they have wasted their time or have they been informed, amused and/or engaged?

When creating anything from a leaflet to a press release, the acronym AIDA (beloved of the life insurance selling fraternity) may be helpful:

- Grab their **Attention.**
- Create **Interest** in your project, from their point of view: 'What's in it for me?'
- Create a **Desire** to get involved.
- Encourage them to take **Action**, as soon as possible, by explaining how and making it as easy as possible for them.

The Press

The nearer to the front page your story is, the more likely it is to be edited, and the more likely you are to get a call from the editor. They may ask you to expand on a controversial or unclear point, so have your answer ready. However, if it is not too controversial, essentially just a story, most local papers take what is sent in and print it verbatim. Always try and get a picture, of the best quality you can manage, to accompany your story. Most local papers now also have a website, which may make it easier to get material published, and will almost certainly allow for greater length. Linking their website story to your Facebook/other social media increases exposure and credibility.

Try to follow up every major thing you do with a press release. Make it easy for the reporters, so they can just cut and paste. Make sure it's clear and easy to see how you can be contacted. Try and develop a relationship with reporters and editors, so you know their real deadlines and they know what is likely to be coming well in advance. That way, you will not be wasting their time.

TV and radio

Seductive though it may be to see yourself on the screen, TV news programmes in particular can be a massive waste of time. Look carefully at them and you will see that local issues are rarely given more than 30 seconds of broadcast time. Hours of careful posing and interviews nearly always seem result in a few seconds of screen time that either fails to get your message across or is positively unhelpful. There are obvious exceptions. In our case the flashmob, mentioned earlier, worked well for local TV. But conversely IfF Councillor Nick White's whole morning spent at studios in Bristol led to just a few moments of bland and unhelpful broadcast.

In general, my advice would be to ignore TV totally unless you have a specific goal in mind, such as voter registration. Live radio interviews can be more useful as you have a little more control, but as before, be wary of edited pieces.

If you are going to use broadcast media, it is essential that you practice what you are going to say and stick to it, politely refusing to answer any unscheduled, 'left field' questions.

When we were campaigning, FromeTV, a local web-based TV, was running; we also have a thriving local FM radio station. Both gave us good coverage that allowed linkage of their output to our Facebook and Twitter pages.

Letters

It is my belief that one of the main things that puts people off anything to do with politics is personal bickering. Local papers, however, love it. The key is to stay positive and never enter into personal attacks. This is incredibly difficult in the face of the nonsense that gets printed. At one point I could not resist a witty three-line comment to the local paper. Next week, there was a whole avalanche of replies, and my one column inch led to pages of free opposition publicity, and plenty of 'told you so' comments.

A key tactic you are likely to face is inspired by a certain Herr Goebbels, who infamously said "If repeated often enough, a lie will become the new truth". Eventually, it may become necessary to counter a repeated untruth – but do it as factually as possible and without personal insult. We also set up a website page to post simple, clear, factual information in order to counter the fiction of opposition. Twitter and Facebook can then link to this in a single line without entering into the mud-slinging.

This approach caused consternation amongst some supporters, who were itching for our responses, and who measured campaign success by column inches, however corrosive. Holding back takes nerve. Disappointingly, we've found in Frome that the ethos has not rubbed off on others: sniping letters and election material based on 100% negativity continue to trickle through the letter box from the political parties.

New media:
Social media and the Internet

Essentially this means Facebook, Twitter, your website and maybe YouTube – with email as a major communication tool. It is important to have all these set up really early on, at least by the time of your first public announcement of the campaign. However, there is a chicken and egg situation here, as you want all the candidates to be involved in selecting a name and creating the media. A temporary Facebook for the first few events is one way to get things going and then morph across to the real thing. If you have under 200 'likes' on Facebook, you can change the name easily. Twitter lets you change it at any point.

Top reasons to use social media are to:

- Stay relevant and up to date.
- Be able to quickly respond.
- Be able to quickly and cheaply invite and organise.
- Maintain ongoing interest.
- Gain feedback.
- Keep in touch with supporters and maintain their enthusiasm.

While social media has the advantage of being able to broadcast information quickly and easily, which can then be repeated and multiplied, it is hard to put forward complex ideas and easy for posts to be misinterpreted, often deliberately by your opposition. It is easy to waste a vast amount of time on these seductive technologies and constant review is necessary to check how much difference you think is really being made. Check the audience you are attracting. You may only be reaching a few people who are not the voters you want to attract. Facebook and websites can provide regular data on how many people are looking at what you put up. Some hosts – such as Wordpress – can give you minute-by-minute updates on views and from where people found the site. Be sure to use this information. Overall, I believe that when used well and carefully, these media can be central to a modern campaign. But, don't forget to keep things in perspective. If you use different Social Media, it's also important to develop a joined-up approach to avoid confusion and/or conflict. Here is how the three major new media compare and potentially complement each other:

Website

- Provides detailed information on the Ways of Working and principles as they emerge.
- Allows full information on candidates.
- Creates an opportunity for deeper debate and gathering opinions.

Facebook

- Allows individuals to make and maintain contact.
- Provides a quick and easy view of what is going on/coming up.
- Points to articles elsewhere.
- Advertises events.

Twitter

- Encourages organisations and individuals to take an interest in your campaign and the local political scene.
- Links you to other organisations.
- Broadcasts your existence.
- Points to and raises awareness of local issues.

YouTube and Vimeo

If you have the contacts and skills. YouTube or Vimeo are great places to put over your own messages as short videos which can link to your website. Taking each of these in turn, what follows aims to provide a newcomer to these forms of social media with the basics that you'll need. By far the best idea is to find someone who already uses them to coordinate this aspect of your campaign.

A clear, simple website is essential in getting information across. Facebook and Twitter can then signal people to it. If Frome is anything to go by, the political parties are likely to only have regional or national websites with little or no information on local candidates. Having an upbeat website with full candidate information and good photos makes a huge difference.

In Frome we initially went for:

- A front page in blog style with articles and debate.
- An 'About Us' page with principles and history linking to a 'Candidates page' and individual candidates' pages.
- A 'Contact Us' page. Email addresses for asking questions, offering support, requesting help for things like placing posters. Links to Facebook and Twitter.
- A 'Register to Vote' page, giving details of how to do so.
- Which ward are you in? A page containing information on how to vote and the different tiers of government.

If you are allowing the public to comment on your site, I recommend two simple rules: be polite, and post under your own name. This will help control 'trolls' and spurious postings. In the event, the IfF candidate's pages, blogs and individual emails weren't much used. However, the site did have significant viewing and undoubtedly added to the impression of a serious group of people operating in the current century. On occasion, we did direct all debate from Facebook and other media (including the newspapers) to the website and then managed an online debate on our terms (see rules above). We tried to raise an issue roughly once a week, aiming to cover all major areas during the campaign.

Facebook can be used in two ways.

Firstly, it can be used organically, with users posting comments and their own articles. This needs to be maintained and 'patrolled' – it is a real downside that both Facebook and Twitter attract an especially noxious line in often personal attacks. You have to be really firm not to retaliate, as it is impossible to win. Staying positive and steering people to clear factual information on the website (where there is no place for 'vandalism') is fine. In Frome we continue to have a steady stream of nonsense, often from outside Frome. The hope is that sane people see the unsubstantiated attacks and your mature response, and add to your support. You do need to be clear on how you will manage challenging comments/posts/discussion topics. It is important to have a lead person to take responsibility for answering. Instant replies are often tempting, but in our experience if you wait a little, a member of the public will often say what you were going to. It's much better coming from someone in the wider community.

> "Some of our more feisty members got drawn into Facebook arguments with Lib Dems supporters which were time consuming and blood pressure raising. Best thing I've learnt is to ignore those not interested in genuine debate just point scoring or plain bullying/bad-mouthing and to be myself in a public role."
>
> *Pippa Goldfinger, IiF councillor*

Secondly, Facebook can be used to develop and build a campaign. This works best for a specific issue with widespread interest.

Although younger people do use Facebook more, there are a growing number of older users amongst the 24m who engage each day in the UK. Perhaps because their parents are becoming more active, youngsters are now increasingly migrating to new phone based apps including WhatsApp, WeChat and KakaoTalk – but we'll deal with this in the second edition. Note well that it is a big mistake to think that a Facebook presence alone will bring younger voters and supporters into the fold: you must have policies that relate to or excite them. I would also recommend having someone savvy managing Facebook and any campaign amongst your supporters – they will need to be able to 'translate' and clarify postings as they are shared.

Use **Twitter** to focus direct traffic to the website and to invite engagement with issues. Twitter can be used to direct followers to events and links, but Twitter etiquette demands that you link to issues of wider interest. Finding someone who can put out a regular stream of Tweets – one or two a day – will build up a following. (Around 6m Twitter users in the UK are looking at their accounts regularly and I note the mayor of Frome has more than 700 followers.)

Youtube and/or **Vimeo** provide potential for posting short video clips straight into Facebook or linking to the website. New technology makes this easier almost by the day. However, unless you have someone who will do this for you, who is already skilled and active, it's unlikely to be worth starting from scratch.

Emails. It is absolutely essential to build and maintain a list of supporters' email addresses.

That means getting legible addresses at every possible opportunity and remembering to feed them key information by email. These people are often your most ardent supporters. Make them feel special. Give them information before the wider world. Consult with them, and then, most importantly, act on their views and feedback. Ask them to do things: in general supporters are looking for ways to support you, so meet their need.

Finally, to return to the key question for all: campaign activity. 'Who is your market?' Make sure the energy you put into these various activities (and any more we didn't think of in Frome) is proportional to potential votes. It may be obvious, but keep your eye on the prize. I've spent hours crafting letters to the paper which have been read and enjoyed by my friends and a handful of others who would have voted for us anyway.

11. Election Day and the Count

The author and Toby Eliot with the 'swingometer' at the count

So, at last, election day dawns. Traditionally the parties put a lot of effort into chasing people who have promised support. They do this through checking off whether known supporters turn up at a polling station and if they don't, phoning them and/or offering a lift. This is especially important for the parties with a key loyal support group, and if the weather is bad. For a group of independents, it is probably more important to just get voter numbers up: the people who weren't going to vote, and new voters. So Facebook-ing and Tweeting, alongside being out and about in public places makes sense.

In Frome, we had a last leaflet drop the day before the poll, with simple, clear messaging about who the candidates were and where to vote. Don't underestimate the levels of apathy and confusion. On the day, you can't campaign near to polling stations, but you can go outside shops, pubs and places like stations where commuters are coming home and voting (or not).

And then – the next day for local elections, through the night for higher levels – there is the count. If at all possible this is worth going to, because it is great theatre, whatever happens. Voting slips are physically put in piles and candidates can see these grow. Eventually, results are declared. This is (among other things) a unique opportunity to learn people's real names as they are read out: the person you always knew as Gerry Smith is actually Gerald Forsythe de Hapsburg Smith. It's also a moment when people's competitive edge and triumphal nature may be hard to hide and naff comments about a 'fair campaign' get made. At the end of the day, you have either personally and as a group won, or not.

Toby Eliot (who is good at these things) made us a spreadsheet and our very own Swingometer, so as figures came in we could instantly analyse what was happening. This added to the occasion, and provided instant info for the press release.

Vote Share			Seats	
IfF	9445	44.97%	IfF	10
Con	5377	25.60%	Con	3
LD	4713	22.44%	LD	4
Lab	1018	4.85%	Lab	0
Ind	448	2.13%	Ind	0
Total Votes	**21001**	**100.00%**	**Total Seats**	**17**

So what now?

Win, lose or draw – the answer is easy: party.

Then, meet to discuss what needs doing with urgency.

If you have won the majority of seats, prepare to govern. If you have not then there will be some decisions to make. You will need to meet soon and decide what's sacrosanct from your Ways of Working and Principles. In other words, what compromises might you be prepared to make to work with a political party or other non-aligned independents to form the biggest group? You may well decide you want to bring some of your non-elected candidates and/or supporters into this conversation.

As a minority group on the council, you may well be able to inspire some real changes, and if there is not an overall majority then you are as much in the mix as anyone. And even if you disengage and do not want to take things further, others may. *Flatpack Democracy* has a blog site, mentioned earlier, and it would be great if you shared your experiences and thoughts if you find yourself in this situation.

Some groups are not tempted to sup with the devil at all. In early 2013 Beppe Grillo's M5S party in Italy won around 25% of the seats in both houses but refused to work with either main party. Following this, M5S have railed against the fragile alliance other parties formed, hoping to gain a greater percentage at the inevitable new election.

In reality at local levels, long nights of hard bargaining to form the largest group are unlikely. As a group of independents such negotiations would be very difficult to hold together. What is more likely is that the largest party or group (with a majority or not) makes recommendations which are then voted on by the all the elected representatives.

More decisions if you don't take power?

If just a few independents are elected, you will need to decide whether this is a bridgehead for next time – as has happened with Bristol Independents' one elected councillor in the city – or whether to simply resign. Resigning as soon as you are elected is not considered 'good form'. It's potentially costly for the council to run a by-election. But if you are quite clear that the whole thing was a failure and there are better things to do in life than wait four years for another try, I'd say do it. I would have done.

And you may be inspired by Robert Burn's writing in the *Declaration of Arbroath,* a declaration of Scottish Independence written in 1320, "If at first you don't succeed, try, try and try again."

And finally, don't forget you have only two weeks to get the signs down and 28 days in which to send in your accounts.

12. That was the Easy Bit

Dickon Moore, Britain's youngest mayor? *Image by Chris Bailey Photography 2014*

The day after the night before.

Congratulations, you've woken up an elected councillor. It's quite likely that you won't really know what that means in real terms. This chapter assumes – and hopes – you are one of a group of independents who have overall control of a council, or enough power to make things happen. It looks at key areas that are important to get a handle on quickly. It also sets out my interpretation of Frome's experience in each area.

Six key areas for speedy attention:

- What's on the immediate horizon: the council's existing schedule of meetings, visits or other commitments?
- Who are the staff – known as 'officers' – and what are their roles?
- What is the structure of the council and its committees?
- How will the council relate to the public?
- What are the rules – known as 'The Standing Orders'?
- What is the current strategy and budget, and what's the timetable for any new ones?

As you start to understand these six things, it will become apparent that there are a number of vital decisions with long-term repercussions, many of which centre on timing. Wait too long and it is very likely you will find yourself falling in with the existing system and endorsing, by default, decisions made by the previous administration. Act too quickly and you risk making rash, ill-informed decisions. We should learn from Tony Blair and his first New Labour government of 1997. They promised to stick with the previous Tory budget and strategy, which undoubtedly played a part in more radical ideas never emerging.

My advice is: don't sign up to anything unless you are happy with it, and delay decisions as long as possible in order to properly understand all of the consequences. Always ask why something is the way it is, or why it is done the way it is done. Much of local government is limping along and needs a huge kick up the arse. Consider ditching the hackneyed adage 'if it ain't broke don't fix it' and replace it with 'if it ain't broke break it'. Go for common sense not common practice. Of course, it depends what kind of mess you are inheriting and the skill-base of you and your staff. In my view, it may well be better in the long term to wipe much of the slate clean and then rebuild in order to get the best outcome for your constituency.

What's on the immediate horizon? The existing schedule of meetings, visits and other commitments.

You'll need to understand staffing, the rules and so on as quickly as possible, and it's important to know what's coming up. There will probably be the main council and some existing committee meetings, and there may also be visits and other council events. We found ourselves with a visitation from Frome's three twin towns before we had any time at all to practice our Polish, French and German.

These formal or 'set piece' occasions are likely to take over the new mayor's life in particular. Staff, if they are set in their ways, may well assume councillors know where to be when, what to wear at the annual duck race, or who needs to be there for the Lord High Sherriff's visit. You need to disabuse them of this assumption very early on in your tenure. For example, no one told us the local MP expected to be invited to the first main meeting, and he was exceedingly cross not to be. It is really important to be firm about what you expect from your officers in these early days, and to make clear what you will and will not do. This will help you to stay in control and not disappear into the 'how it's always been done' vortex.

Who are the staff and what are their roles?

What staff there are depends on the size of the council. The smallest will have a part-time town clerk to support the council with legal requirements and running meetings.

The largest will have a vast structure headed by a chief executive. In either case, their key roles are to ensure the councillors (confusingly known as 'members') understand their roles and duties, and don't break the law. If logistically possible, meeting them all (including any grounds staff that are likely to be stuck in a distant park and never meet anyone) is an important first step.

Who the town clerk or chief executive is, and their attitude to your aims is incredibly important. It's an odd role, given that their management – and sometimes their complete direction of travel – changes every four years. They hold a vast amount of power, especially in their knowledge of the rules and of council and town history. Some will want to help you in every way possible, while for others, their role is a tool of control. In Frome, we started with a chief executive who openly stated that he saw his job as "to protect Frome from you lot". He left not long afterwards. One of our key mistakes was not to be braver in ensuring that, from the outset, he understood that we expected his full support in all matters.

> "The relationship between leading councillors and senior staff in local government is probably the most complex and potentially the most fraught of any in the private or public sector. Unless this leadership group can forge an honest and transparent understanding on values, principles and aspirations, there is only a slim chance that the council they lead can be anything other than mediocre."
>
> *Mel Usher, IfF councillor*

When you know what you want to achieve (see the Strategy section below), you may well want to hold a staff review. Many council staff have done much the same thing for many years, wryly watching new sets of incompetent councillors bumble in and out. Their management, motivation and responsibility are all minimal. To achieve your lofty ambitions, you need these people on board. Our experience was that the vast majority are basically competent, and once set free with recognition and a major say in what happens, they will blossom.

Of course there will be councils with excellent inspiring staff and, equally, there will be some people who are so set in their ways no amount of support will get them where you want. I believe that the key ethos has to be around instinctively saying 'Yes'. This doesn't always come easily. If there are still councillors who are deeply traditional or set in a mould of negativity, this won't help: it reduces the chances that the staff will change. I've been astonished in Frome at the way some councillors managed to retain their perpetual grump while success stared them in the face, along with opportunities to contribute and enjoy their role.
Some astute additions and changes may be essential to move the ship forward. We carried

out a staff review in the first few months, using an external consultant. In some ways this was too early: we made a mess of not explaining our intentions, and some staff saw it as threat to their employment, so it took a while to recover. If a staff review recommends that a post is not required, redundancies can be made (with associated costs). What you cannot do is then recreate that post (or something close to it) and appoint a new person. Basically, you can't use staff reviews as a way to get rid of an individual: just a post.

It is also important to know and understand the importance of the various qualifications staff have and don't have. Especially of the 'Statutory and Proper Officer' aka the clerk or chief executive. Anyone can have this role within a parish council, with no qualifications required. To be accredited as a 'Quality Council', the clerk needs to have the CiLCA qualification. Becoming a Quality Council '...demonstrates an ability to deliver efficient services to local residents and speak with greater authority to principal councils when seeking delegated functions which can be better carried out locally'. In addition, if the council wants to use the General Power of Competence (under the Localism Act), the Proper Officer needs to have passed an additional and new section of the CiLCA qualification. This General Power means the council can do anything as long as it is not illegal, or involves raising an army or taxes: it may be very important in taking some actions. Frome's new town clerk gained this qualification, allowing us to move to Competence (from incompetence?). So, having a look at qualifications alongside skills and experience will be important – not just to spot shortfalls, but to recognise talent and then work with and manage people well.

Not surprisingly, staffing is all a hugely sensitive and tricky area. There will be personnel support and advice either from within your own council, or the tiers above. In Frome we moved to take out two layers of management and consolidate a chief executive and deputy into a town clerk. It took us around two years to achieve a structure with a very flat management team and three tiers replacing five. We have brought in two new staff with jobs that support community initiatives, rather than carry out tasks on behalf of the community. Overall staff costs are only marginally higher than when we were elected. And crucially, after the changes had bedded in, the longest serving worker in Frome Town Council described the atmosphere as "...the best it's been in 20 years..."

What is the structure of the council and its committees?

As with staffing, this will obviously depend on the size and history of the council. With larger bodies it is very likely to be more set and less easy to change. The first thing will be to understand what the committees are, their mandates and how their membership is determined. It is usual for committee membership to reflect the political balance of the councillors, although this can be waived by any group, and/or they don't have to nominate someone. It is also likely that the very first thing a new council will be asked to do is to propose committee membership, including chairs and vice chairs – with the new mayor chairing main meetings.

This is a key moment to PAUSE and not be rushed into decisions. What the committees are and where the power lies is clearly crucial. For this reason there will be much tension and upset at any suggestion of change – it's quite likely Councillor X has chaired planning for 20 years and he's very clear who is an expert in planning. The initial decisions that you must consider relate to: 1) what committees to have 2) who should sit on them and 3) who should chair them. Depending on the rules, you may or may not be able to change things quickly. Whether you have a majority or not, you can carefully work out who should sit on what committees. Make sure your group of independents has a majority wherever possible. The chair and deputy will be elected at the first meeting of each committee, so there is less pressure on that front. In smaller councils, the deputy will only have a role in the absence of the chair, so it may be an opportunity to bring people not in your group into the fold, or to recognise their experience

Choosing the mayor sounds like a big decision and the role can be an arduous one. We chose to separate the 'public face of the council' role (opening events and being out in the community) from that of elected Leader of the Council, who is spokesperson in terms of the council's business. The mayor is, however, the face associated with the work of the council, and can say a lot about who you are. We went first for Nick White, who was already well known in Frome and was game to raise the public profile of the mayor. This sent a clear message of change and a positive upbeat approach to life. All three IfF Frome mayors so far have spoken of what a brilliant experience it has been, and have built upon a high level of engagement established by the previous Liberal Democrat mayor.

In Frome, we had a plethora of committees, some secret, most with very few members. 60% of the Deputy Chief Executive's time was spent on writing agendas and minutes. Therefore, we suspended the committee structure in order to give time to rebuild something more suited to Frome and this century. We made this shift at the annual town meeting, because it preceded the first full town council meeting when decisions would otherwise have been made. Tears were shed, doom and disaster was predicted and, rather sweetly, we were accused of rash incompetence. In Liskeard, their similar move was met with the town clerk's outrage and bluster – but new councillors had read their Standing Orders (see below) and knew what could be done.

In my view, the anger in Frome was in part because the remaining politicians were in shock at IfF's victory. We underestimated the hurt this caused them. In Bristol, the newly-elected independent mayor George Ferguson said "They may hate each other but they hate you more because you're showing them up." For six months after he was elected, Labour councillors refused to join his cross party cabinet.

In Frome, we replaced the previous committee structure with just two: The External Affairs Committee, which deals with everything that the council does not have direct control over, and the Internal Affairs Committee, which deals with things like staffing, the budget and upkeep of land that the council manages. There is just one sub-committee: Planning. Internal and External committees meet every two months, as does the main council (with a Planning meeting every three weeks to match in with the district cycles). This took a while to settle down, as people worked out which committee does what, and we sought a balance of public participation and results, but it now functions excellently.

> Some found the changes easier than others: "I am writing because I lost the will to live and escaped at the break. The external affairs agenda was too long... The fault is due to all the previous number of committees being condensed into a single committee meeting, when there is too much business to attend to. What a mess."
>
> *Adrian Dobinson, Frome Liberal Democrat councillor*

> "Re: External Affairs Meeting: What a boring title I have just typed, to what turned out to be a really inspiring meeting last night! It was just the sort of town council meeting I always felt should happen, which involved residents and their concerns and dreams for their home patch. What joy and well done to the IfFy lot!"
>
> *Frome resident Jacqueline Peverly.*

> And later: "As a lawyer, one can sometimes get over-excited about the minutiae of procedure, so please excuse this letter if that is what you think I am doing. Having been to two meetings of the External Affairs Committee, I applaud the attempt to improve the proces... I particularly welcome the arrangement to enable people to comment on particular agenda items at the time those items appear in the agenda."
>
> *Frome resident Neil Howlett*

> Neil went on to ask for clarity on who can and who cannot speak, and when.

The way councillors function and the structure of the council morphs into the next section on how the Council as a whole relates to the public.

From the website information following IfF's demolition of the previous committee structure:

> "The previous committee structure was outdated and outmoded. There were too many layers, and issues get shoehorned into committees and sub-committees that may not be best placed to deal with them. We need a system that allows councillors to make fast, positive decisions based on sound advice and expertise from within the community. We also need a system that allows Frome residents to see clearly how any one decision is made."
>
> *Toby Eliot, IfF councillor*

Part of a conversation the author had with a prospective Derbyshire councillor:
A potential candidate I met in Derbyshire went to a council meeting and sat at the back. When the Chair noticed him, he asked:
"I'm sorry, what are you doing here?"
To which he replied:
"I'm a member of the public, I thought that was allowed."
"Yes it is, it's just never happened before."

How will the council relate to the public?

Earlier in this guide I set out why I believe a fundamental change is required in the relationship between councillors and council staff, and with the wider population that they aim to represent and serve. We must forge better links with the community, and this means engaging with people in new ways, so that they can see the real changes that their interaction has bought about. I believe sharing the load with the electorate is the only way democracy can survive and thrive.

The most obvious place to start is with meetings. Traditionally there were very few members of the public attending – although we have a core of three loyal women who come to them all. Simpler, more open committee structures are much easier for the public to access and understand. We've reduced formality greatly for example by encouraging the use of first names, not titles, and by distributing homemade biscuits. As chair, I make a considerable effort to introduce councillors and staff and explain who can and can't speak at the start of each meeting (and then try to be flexible in applying the rules). We regularly invite community groups to speak before a meeting: this has been great in opening up meetings but a nightmare in trying to keep people to short presentations.

We advertise and promote meetings on Facebook and with posters, using plain English agendas. While the official agenda has to retain key legal features, the public poster advertising it can be as wacky as you like. We follow up after meetings with Facebook and email plain English summaries of key points (you need to be careful in summarising before minutes are agreed, but Facebook seems to provide a grey area that allows for this). This approach has brought very large numbers to the Annual Meetings, and is slowly encouraging more to committee meetings. Personally, I remain frustrated at the small numbers but am having to recognise that many people elect councillors to make their decisions for them. They are generally happy to be kept informed without having to come to yet another meeting on a cold winter's night (however good the biscuits are).

Dragging council meetings into this century can be a battle. Newly-elected Open Liskeard councillor Rachel Brooks began knitting in their first meeting, only to be accused of being disrespectful to both the council and the Liskeard electorate. A councillor supporting Rachel was then "told to stand when addressing the council." Systematic belittling of those outside the system is endemic.

As an aside, I am deeply proud that the first official complaint to the new council related to my wearing shorts to a meeting (despite the fact that they were my very clean ones). For the record, I was also wearing an impressively ironed shirt. We took on board the criticism and four of us wore shorts to the next meeting.

> "You couldn't have had a better example of how not to engage with people than the recent 'Meet the Mendip Cabinet' at the Cheese and Grain. Poorly advertised and badly planned, it was a disaster, sucking all of the life out of the room and leaving most people frustrated and angry. They even brought their own bouncer in case the locals turned ugly! Compare that to the Frome Annual Town Meeting, when 140 people turned out to celebrate successes and where the last people there after three hours of discussion had to be (politely) asked to leave. Or the packed Steiner School meeting, where different views were shared amicably amongst the 'fors' and 'againsts'. Simple examples, but all adding up to a philosophy of engagement, collaboration and 'can do'."
>
> *Mel Usher, IfF councillor*

To be honest, in many cases the base line for good behaviour and public engagement is so low that any change will be an improvement. For example:

> "After the debacle that was last week's Shepton Mallet Annual Town Meeting (when all of us are supposed to have a chance to air views and raise issues of public concern), I wonder if Shepton is turning into a police state... It's only recently that some councillors thought fit to send the police round to warn off a resident in his 80s... last Tuesday the same group of councillors again called in the police at the annual town meeting that descended into pantomime..."
>
> *Garfield Kennedy, Shepton Mallet councillor.*

In Frome, we also developed the concept of formal Working Parties. I believe that an essential part of the ethos of independents is that the council should recognise and support the energy and skills of people within the town.

On specific issues, so far including open spaces, ethics, bicycling and walking routes and sports provision, we have invited members of the public to recommend policy and strategy. Councillors may be there because of an expertise they have in the topic to be discussed, but otherwise are actively discouraged. Tight Terms of Reference for the group are defined first, and the meetings are limited in time to usually three meetings of two hours over a six week period. The recommendations are taken to the council, which will adopt them unless there is a really clear and good reason not to do so – failure to follow this principle would rapidly undermine the whole idea. IfF believes that this method of working uses the skills and local knowledge of the community; it brings more people into the workings of the council and it augments the skills of councillors and council staff. Where the Working Parties have functioned best is when they have a skilled independent chair/facilitator, participants who are prepared to do as well as talk, and a member of council staff able to quickly respond and to support recommendations.

> "The attitude we have, that the established parties never did, is that just because we're elected it doesn't mean we know everything", ruminates Dave Anderson, a builder and councillor for the Frome Keyford ward; "Top-down governance doesn't work at the local level – it's the people who live in Frome that know what's best for the area."
>
> From 'What a democratic revolution in a Somerset town could teach our political class'
> *The Independent,* 12th November 2012.

We also commissioned a paid facilitator to bring together Participation Week. During this we:

- Brought in national expertise on public engagement to run workshops for the voluntary sector.
- Sent people into different areas of the town to ask focussed questions like 'What do you like best about Frome and why?' and 'name one thing you would change in Frome!'
- Set up a soap box so people could share their views.
- Organised a mass public town clean up.
- Established links into the Neighbourhood Planning consultation.
- Launched a young peoples' consultation, with other events already planned.
- Wrapped up the whole Participation Week with a town meeting.

Participate Frome's Facebook site had more interest in those ten days than the Council's has had in two years. A key thing we learned was that by not being seen as 'The Council', far more people were happy to engage. We'll be incorporating the lessons learned during this week regarding our relationship to the public from now on. Indeed, this kind of approach, alongside a realisation that the business meetings of the council will never really excite the masses, may well be a sensible way forward. For example, in the Icelandic capital Reykjavik, they accept that only a few people will attend council meetings, and with 80% of the population using Facebook, understand that that's where the 24-hour-a-day political engagement is.

Two other specific ideas to broaden engagement that we used in Frome are:

- A 'citizen's panel' for the Neighbourhood Plan consultation, whereby a cross section of the community are paid to come to meetings to express their views.

- An effort to really boost the focus and engagement with young people, which particularly involved our 22-year-old mayor, Dickon Moore. Through a youth organisation in the town, a Mayor and Deputy for Young People were elected. It was one of their jobs to support Dickon in his work. They are treated as much as possible as full councillors, attending and speaking at all meetings.

We see this as another work in progress towards extending reach into the community.

Reducing formality, enforcing plain English, embracing social media: all of these can be adopted immediately by parish and town councils. We are often told that people are sick of politics and politicians: but is it the other way around? Our experience in Frome is that people are very willing to engage, but only at a very local level where they can see a problem and can grasp a solution. Hundreds of people have turned out to discuss the pros and cons of a Steiner school, access to a local meadow, and to whether a new supermarket would be positive or negative. Traditionally, politicians pretend to welcome people but deep down perhaps they just want to turn them away. They correctly see people as awkward, messy, unpredictable and not respectful enough of their status.

Giving power to local people to define broad areas of development has been central to Frome's development of a Neighbourhood Plan, and as part of 'Localism'. This has turned into a much larger task than expected, and has included a high level of proper, time consuming, consultation. It will finish with a referendum which will require more than 50% of voters to approve it before implementation. However, the process will have really engaged with a great range of people who will then clearly see that their time and effort has led to the concrete action which they desire.

There are some great organisations such as Involve ("experts in public participation... who believe passionately in a democracy where citizens are able to take and influence the decisions that affect their lives") and some excellent techniques for public engagement. We've used 'World Cafe' and 'Open Space' sessions to move things on light years from turgid meetings with a line of 'experts' and the usual suspects asking the usual questions. Again, you must bring in a facilitator (or train council staff) with skills in these areas, especially when there is a contentious or 'hot' issue where views are polarised. This will take time and while it is happening, there are very likely to be local plans and strategies on which to start work in the meantime.

In keeping with the desire to maintain ongoing engagement, tell people what you are up to. The IfF council's first strategic document is easily readable – it imagined Frome four years ahead and then identified what decisions would need to be made over what time to achieve this future state. The document formed the base of activity and budgeting for three years and its novel approach captured the interest of the regional media. (The 2011-2015 Strategy for Success is available from the council website and the Flatpack blog).

The standing orders.

These are the rules under which the council operates. They include what meetings should be held when, how many people should be on each committee, under what circumstances someone can be asked to leave a meeting, and so on. They may be weighty and incredibly boring, but it's important to have an early look, and then quickly try and find someone to really unpick them. There will be some parts set in national law which you can't do much about, but the vast majority is up to you to accept or change.

The person who really knows the rules can be a boon or a total pain. At a recent meeting, the invitation (known as a 'summons') didn't have the time on it. If someone had wanted, they could have declared the whole meeting and all decisions void under Standing Orders. You can be very vulnerable with a Standing Orders nerd against you. The best approach is to hugely simplify the rules, which reduces the risk of abuse, and, more importantly, makes the process open to both councillors and the public. This is an area we started work on in Frome but have not revisited for far too long.

What current strategies and budget are in place and what is the timetable for the new ones?

It may well be that the council is operating a three or five year strategy that you are part way through. There will also be a mass of 'strategies' at other levels – district and county, for example – and some which are specific, such as economic and regeneration plans. You may already have a Neighbourhood Plan at some stage of its adoption. In Frome, there had been a fairly recent community plan, funded and with a report produced containing solid coverage of the main issues that people cared about. As a group, you probably made various promises of action in election material. How do your aspirations link in to existing plans and budgets? The town clerk/chief executive should be able to talk you through all of this, and explain the interactions. They provide parameters that you will need to act within. Also, funding may well be attached to particular aspects of plans, i.e. if you cut the activity, you will lose the funding. There will be opportunities, but also constraints that you can't escape from, at least initially.

In general, it seems that people like to be consulted regarding broad direction, by being presented with a number of contrasting but viable options. The 'tell us what you think' approach can create unworkable expectations/dreams, unless it's part of a clear process. People often want you, as their elected representatives, to define a range of possible actions. They do, however, want to be brought back into the picture to confirm that you are heading in the right direction and crucially, they want to be kept in the loop in terms of how things are going.

Wherever possible, strategic direction should be based on such an ongoing methodology. What really pisses people off is being asked an opinion, then never hearing anything about the issue again or, worse yet, having their opinion ignored. The sham consultation is one of the main reasons that people get infuriated with government, and ultimately disengage. As is too often heard by a frustrated public, "What's the point in getting involved in a consultation – they just do what they were going to do anyway!"

'Surveys' that are really just an excuse for weighted questions and go nowhere are another bone of contention. One example "Was the town council right to raise council tax by 23% this year?" (From a Liberal Democrat election leaflet for 2013 County Council elections). Results from these phoney surveys are almost never published, and if they are, involve flagrant abuse of statistics which alienates voters: "Our survey of 210 people asked, "Are you happy with the proposed tax rise? The results showed that 20,550 Frome residents are not happy." (a Tory letter to the local paper). This kind of activity just gives politics a bad name, as it is so blatantly ridiculous.

> "For the first time in 25 years of living in Frome, I feel that the town council is openly accessible to me as an individual, and actively seeks to engage with the people of Frome."
>
> *Nicky Fleming, Frome resident*

So, the first few weeks are likely to be hectic. It is, however, really important to grasp any nettles presented quickly and firmly. If you let the old ways re-establish themselves, they will be much harder to shift. Even knowing this, I have been surprised at how easy it is to slip into 'council speak' and to not bother with the homemade biscuits.

Of course, there is the truism that all power corrupts. Or at least, it tries to. The next chapter looks at exactly this – how do you retain the energy, stick to your ideals and meet the excessive expectations of your supporters?

13. Keeping the Show on the Road

Postcards from the campaign about Frome's public toilets

Some months later, the initial chaos of change has diminished. The opposition has joined in, stopped coming, or developed their own style of increasingly irrelevant grump. In Frome's case, they have tried all three and the parties move between them on a six monthly rotation. The staff are either still there or not, with those remaining getting the idea and starting to blossom in new ways. New employees have arrived, bringing with them fresh experience and enthusiasm.

Meanwhile, your 'supporters' will probably all have disappeared. Amongst your own councillors, the pattern of engagement, either 'turning up every few months and not answering emails' to 'going to every meeting possible and sending endless links and emails' is becoming clear. In this, we were no different from any other group of councillors. The feted Way of Working will either be working or it won't. Someone is likely to have emerged as a leader, whether you call them that or not. While you had a reason to work together to get elected, now you will have different ideas on issues. You will probably find aspects of other peoples' personalities difficult. You are after all a group of busy individual carrying out what is,, at most levels of government, a voluntary role.

> "As Woody Allen once said, 80% of success is turning up. And we have turned up and are willing to have a go."
>
> *Mel Usher, IfF councillor.*

As I write, we've fairly recently had our second IfF birthday party (motto: "we're not a party but we do party"). Half way through our first term of office, we have disagreed and we have voted against each other. However, despite predictions, we have continued to work as a group, and I would argue that this council has achieved more in two years than any of its predecessors did. We have now reached a point where we have confident staff who are operating in an environment where they feel able to take sensible risks and make good decisions. Within the constraints of our limited skills and time, a core of councillors are well engaged and making solid, well-informed decisions. 'Yes' is heard more often than 'No', and many more members of the public have positive working links to Frome Town Council. We've not been afraid of tough decisions, for example raising the precept (locally raised tax) in the first year, which was not popular but gave us the funds to meet our ambitions. It's not been perfect, but we have come a long, long way.

So, for us as a group, what have been the key elements in this achievement? Not surprisingly, they link back to the 'Essentials for Election', particularly in terms of how the group works together: using people with a specialism to champion that particular topic, using a facilitator, keeping things light and maintaining our relationship with our supporters. A general point that runs throughout our workings, and which I can't emphasise too much, is that learning to listen is much more important than speaking. Perhaps partly because of that focus on listening, the two councillors with the least confidence two years ago are now mayor and deputy mayor. This gives a huge positive message for others looking in from the outside, as well as for those involved and the rest of the group. This is key to why we have not imploded: we have been looking out, not in.

Taking each of the 'essentials' in turn:

The Ways of Working.

We aren't rigid about these. We still consistently remind each other to move on from issues where a decision has been made, returning to Peit Hein and his statement that "The noble art of losing face may one day save the human race". We tend not to engage in minor disputes where it is clear someone else has either greater interest or more knowledge. It's been about looking for consensus and agreement and always having wider interests of Frome as the bottom line. As a group, we have used an external facilitator for any particularly tricky issue which contains polarised views – not to change those views, but to ensure that everyone is heard. This is a radical change to the way that most politics works, where every opportunity is taken to score points, even if the issue really doesn't matter. Indeed, in our struggles with the highly politicised district council, we find that they prefer to 'lose' than retreat from their position. In other words, they will do anything other than see us 'win', even if that means that they lose too. We try to do things differently.

We have recently been engaged in a by-election, and the Ways of Working were central to attracting and selecting a candidate. The choice was made by a group of individuals who have followed IfF but were not councillors: we deliberately wanted to encourage further diversity, but were also clear that they needed to be prepared to operate within our Ways of Working.

Specialisms.

It is human nature that people are more likely to put time and energy into areas about which they feel strongly and/or have particular skills. Giving a lead in different areas to key people, then really respecting their views and thoughts, can change the dynamic of the group. The downside of this is that whoever takes the lead can be left to carry most of the burden – this has certainly been true of the creation of Frome's Neighbourhood Plan, where the lead person was both tired and had contributed too much of their personal time. We've also brought in challenging experts in particular fields – critical friends who, for example, can take us through elements of the Localism Bill.

Keeping it light.

We hold monthly meetings as a group in someone's house. These are always, whatever the issue at hand, a pleasure to be at. Chairing is very light, with numerous digressions into stories and gossip. Not everyone drinks. These meetings do cover council business and are the fermenting pot of ideas that take us well beyond normal parish council aspirations. We don't exercise control by fixing the agenda items. We do discuss big issues, and sometimes this brings out who is likely to support an issue in a future council meeting. Mostly we agree, not because we are 'a party' but because we reach consensus through well informed decision making.

Keeping it light can, and should, spread into both the group and the council's communication. We've tried hard, and made slow progress at ensuring agendas, the website and regular newsletters are written in plain English. Some of this is frustratingly slow, for example, we identified the need for a new website three years ago and it has still not happened. (And probably by wishing to be flexible and responsive we have inadvertently changed priorities and at times been hard to work with.)

Old agenda:

1 Public participation.

2 For Information – Outstanding Actions.

New agenda:

1 Questions, comments and information from the public.

2 A quick review on previous actions and what is coming up next time..

Acts of Creative Disruption.

Acts of Creative Disruption can play a key role: serious intent and actions do, indeed, often speak louder than words. Frome has the significant disadvantage of being geographically in the corner of both the district and the county, and therefore out on a limb. And at both these levels of government there are large Tory majorities, but only one Tory councillor at each level from Frome. While this does give us something to rail against, it imposes a limit on what we have significant influence over. If you are in a unitary authority (for example the City of Bath) you are more or less answerable directly to central government, which makes it harder for local PR stunts to have any effect. But Frome can be – and needs to be – heard by the layers of government 'above' us.

So it has been our pleasure to remind the district and county of their duties by encouraging or taking part in a number of small but effective 'PR stunts'. All of these also established us a group prepared to do things and take risks, for example:

- Gnomes protesting that Frome wants its own trees during a district tree planting ceremony – in response to their clear refusal to allow Frome to pay for and plant trees within the district owned car park.
- Creating postcards showing 'Frome's architectural heritage' in the form of the district owned, vandalised toilets. This action inspired a local entrepreneur to take on one block of toilets and convert them to a (small) cafe and set of art galleries.
- Where the county council had replaced beautiful and historic paving slabs with tarmac in a conservation area, a group of IfF councillors (under the management of Councillor Dave, a builder), put back the paving slabs. Interestingly, the immediate reaction from the county council was threats and anger, but later on they quietly reversed the policy.

Facilitation.

We've consistently used facilitators in IfF meetings and some council meetings. We've also used this support at the 'IfF Party Conference'. This is not really a 'Party Conference', but more of a party and a conference. Each year we have booked a cottage for the weekend and taken the time away to build our personal relationships, look at some big issues, reflect and review. At one level, a parish council annual 'conference' at the councillors' own expense seems mad. However, it brings together a number of strands of this guide, namely: if you are going to do it, do it well, have ridiculously high aspirations and have fun. I believe that this attitude will help revitalise the moribund state of local 'democracy'. It will help attract people with energy, ideas and enthusiasm who want to be challenged and inspired. This will in turn attract others to engage in a broad democratic movement, and to enjoy their engagement.

One example of the benefit of using a facilitator was well illustrated at our second birthday party, to which all supporters and Frome residents were invited. The walls had large signs with 'I agree', 'I agree with reservations', 'I disagree' and 'I disagree with reservations'. The facilitator made statements such as "IfF has exceeded my expectations." And the 60 or so people present positioned themselves near one of the signs and talked briefly to someone in their group about why they were there. It was very illuminating, quick, light and physical. And it also highlighted some really useful information for us as a group.

> "First of all, let me say how brilliant IfF is – and therefore the ten of you are... and no I have not got your stamina and will not stand in the next round of elections, but I will do all I can to be actively supportive."
>
> *Clare Hein, Frome resident, feedback at the birthday party.*

(Interestingly, to date Clare's contribution has been not so much to IfF directly, but by expertly chairing Working Parties.)

An example of what happens without a facilitator was the 'meeting from hell'. This was an attempt by town and district councils to bring councillors from all levels of local government together, to co-ordinate action on key issues. As Frome Town Council, we had no control over this meeting – so a traditional meeting in every respect (the seating, chairing, agenda, and participants) was all imposed upon us. It ended in acrimony and insults, as party agendas and petty point scoring emerged. This served as a painful reminder that we should not get drawn into situations that our experience and instinct tell us just won't work. One aim of 'Participation Week' (see Chapter 8) was that the public, having experienced real participation, would never allow this sort of exclusive, macho exercise to take place again.

Supporters and keeping in touch.

The second year birthday party was partly for us to celebrate survival, but much more about the future. The initial supporters had, understandably and as predicted, melted away after our election. They may bask in the glow of association, but they haven't especially engaged with what we are doing. We now realise that IfF has been pathetic at communicating our successes. The excuses (that we are too busy doing it, or it's not our interest or skill set) are not really valid.

IfF has enjoyed consistent support from the local newspapers, in the sense that they print our pieces and every now and then say they something positive without being prodded. However, we realise that it's up to us to provide them with the content. We've taken a possibly foolish stance, in re-election terms, to trust the good people of Frome to make the links between the success of the Council and its initiatives, and the presence of IfF. We are encouraging the Council to inform the press, at every opportunity, of its successes. We also decided not to put out a midterm leaflet claiming Council achievements as IfF's because this is what the political parties do.

It is hard to stick to this policy of not proclaiming our achievements loud and long and at every opportunity. It is especially difficult when the parties still chip away with negativity, and lay claim to policies, ideas and activity whether it is true or not. Time will tell if this bold stance was politically suicidal.

Interestingly, we have seen emergence of 'IfFnet' – an independent group of residents who are starting to work on getting the IfF message out to the citizens of Frome. They have already taken over our little used Facebook account and started work on the website.

IfFnet's statement of purposes:
We comprise a small committee that will formulate strategies and coordinate activities in support of two important goals.

Goal 1: The committee's two-year goal is to re-elect an independent council in Frome in 2015. Our strategies are to raise community awareness about the value of having elected an independent council in 2011, increase the database of IfF supporters and recruit volunteers, and identify potential independent candidates for future elections in Frome.

Goal 2: In the longer term, the committee will work to set up a free-standing, volunteer structure to support independent elections in Frome far beyond 2015.

While hugely welcome, this raises some interesting questions, currently unanswered, around the link between IfF councillors and IfFNet:

Do the two need to speak with a common voice?

Can IfFNet influence policy more directly than other community members?

Do the supporters of IfFNet have a role in deciding candidates next time round? (If not, who does?)

These questions raise other fundamental issues around how IfF retains its identity as a group of individuals working together, while also taking on facets of a party… or not.

It was the initial surge of supporters that gave the 'founding group' the courage to launch IfF. We have always been clear that the councillors are only one part of a wider 'movement'. It is also central to our ethos that the council encourages and expands genuine participation. What this raises is where the boundaries of IfF, council and public lie. In an ideal world, we'd all be skipping along happily with the same aims and aspirations, but we haven't yet created that ideal world. IfFNet is a welcome, interesting (and slightly surprising) initiative and the *Flatpack Democracy* blog will keep you up to date on how it is all panning out.

One of the key roles that supporters (and potentially IfFnet) can play is that of 'critical friends'. As such they are part of the essential activity of assessing what's been done and helping to design what lies ahead. They can become the core of wider public engagement that the IfF ethos seeks. All too often, councils operate with strategies which, once completed, are never looked at again. An initial plan and budget is only a guess at what is necessary in order to achieve what's required. They need constant monitoring and periodic evaluation. By this, I mean an ongoing assessment of how you are doing against what was planned, and a much deeper analysis of whether the strategy holds up, every few years. If you do this using a range of engaging and exciting methods of participation, you not only get answers to questions, but it helps draw a wider range of people into the process. We've not been nearly strong enough at this, though feedback from 'Participation Week' has allowed us to focus on various issues and gauge the extent to which people feel they have been heard, achieved or still need to be addressed.

> "The ultimate solution is to make your own mind up and go with your own opinion. You were elected because you were of 'independent thought', and the electorate of Frome trusted you to make the right decisions for them. Most people simply cannot be bothered to keep thinking about twinning or council fireworks, unless they're a bit pissed in the pub. Most of us just expect to be allowed to vote once every four years, that's all. The real

role of an elected town councillor is to provide a moral steer for the town. Show me some real leadership and take us in the direction you think is best for us. If it's good for you, then that's fine for me. This above all: 'To thine own self be true, / And it must follow, as the night the day, / Thou cans't not then be false to any man'."

(W Shakespeare) Richard Porteus, IfF candidate.

Re-election.

The dinosaurs are not dead but sleeping: it is clear that the parties will want to re-emerge in a few years. We've seen from their behaviour at county elections and the town by-election that whatever IfF has done for the people of Frome is irrelevant compared to their desire for power.

In December 2013, there was a local by-election for a seat on the town council. This was a relatively meaningless situation, in which IfF would retain a majority whatever happened and anyway there was a full election due in 16 months. Where else would a by-election be contested at all? In fact, the Tories, Liberal Democrats and IfF all had to conduct selection processes to choose candidates. On cold wet evenings just before Christmas, the local MP along with councillors from both within and outside Frome all campaigned hard. Obviously IfF didn't campaign hard enough, coming third behind the winning Lib Dems and the Tories. This was both a warning for IfF, and clear demonstration that just by existing the independent group has increased the visibility and importance of the town council.

14. What Next for Frome and what can we Learn?

The IfF Flyer 'Look What We've Started'

This chapter starts with examples of specific things we have achieved in Frome, then goes on to look at whether our experiences are potentially replicable. I then look at whether these ideas and actions can be replicated nationally, or only at local levels. Hopefully the examples will inspire you but be aware Frome is a work in progress and as yet there are no definitive answers. A more detailed list of achievements can be found in Appendix 2

The speedy creation and unexpected success of IfF in Frome created civic leadership with ambitions far beyond those of a parish council. Without the blinkers of experience, this has enabled us to achieve way above the norm. As we come up against district councillors, seemingly united in their opposition, we have had to recognise there are limits to our ambition. I wonder whether this opposition springs from their own spectacular lack of ambition or just the establishment's dislike of anything new and radical. Either way, I maintain it is vital to push those limits all the time because you need to know if more could be done.

The underlying ethos of all our actions is to build confidence and facilitate opportunity. This we feel is the best way to attract interest and investment in our town. The highest profile example of this is the monthly market. Thousands of people now visit the Town for the market. This brings significant benefit to local shops and an important 'feel good' factor for everyone. While IfF councillors pushed and supported this to happen, for example in facilitating the closure of the relevant streets, we were acting as individual enthusiasts for our community, without secondary political motives. The market management has now been handed to an independent organisation and we can move on to the next project.

An atmosphere of achievement and ambition breeds more of the same. In Frome this was well illustrated by an early approach we had from a local philanthropist. He wanted to fund projects that focussed on the less well off and those that strengthen the local community. This led to the setting up of the Frome Development Community Interest Company (FDCIC) with the private donor pledging £250,000 over five years. Having significant funding in place has meant that FDCIC can leverage matched funding for projects from the likes of the Big Lottery. One example is the purchase of land for 100 new allotments, reducing the waiting list from ten years to virtually nothing. The council shared the costs and ownership has been transferred to a charity specifically set up to benefit the people of Frome. FDCIC has also spawned a separate jointly funded project – Fair Frome – to work on issues related to poverty such as support for the local credit union, food bank and emergency housing. Not every town will have this good fortune but it is absolutely clear that IfF's approach encouraged and enabled these significant outcomes. Now the infrastructure is in existence, there is the potential to attract further private support.

Similarly, the council's initial investment in photovoltaic panels and the purchase of an electric vehicle for the grounds staff played a major role in showing we were serious about sustainable issues and could deliver on projects. This energy focus has led on to a joint venture between the council, community group Sustainable Frome and Bath and West Community Energy to set up Frome Renewable Energy Co-operative (FRECo).

This is a Community Benefit Society whose aim is to provide a vehicle for local people to invest in, and get a reasonable return from, renewable energy projects with the surplus going to a Community Fund. It has already initiated other energy projects such as Frome Open Homes, a weekend showcasing cost and carbon saving measures throughout Frome. FRECo is a perfect example of the council meeting its strategic aims by enthusiastically and actively supporting highly skilled local volunteers, rather than waiting for them to queue up and beg for help.

We have also not shied away from spending and borrowing. This is partly because the reality of the current low rates of interest means that the Council's savings and un-earmarked reserves are actually loosing value with inflation. We believe they are better spent now to create long-term value and opportunity. Borrowing rates are exceptionally low and opportunities for councils are far greater than individuals or companies. A good example of this is the council's recent £500,000 loan to revamp the Cheese and Grain community building. This has enabled us to exchange a £35,000 p.a. subsidy to interest repayments of around £25,000 p.a. while also supporting a previously struggling business model to exploit exciting, new opportunities. This business model recently won the Cheese and Grain £20K in a bank competition.

All this springs from our strong ethos of Localism. The majority of voters in Frome have probably hardly noticed any changes at all, and proper participation is a ten-year project not a four-year one. But we have started this process and made real inroads. Perhaps this is best demonstrated by the huge Social media engagement in Participation Week and in the December 2013 Frome by-election mentioned earlier.

There will always be some people who confuse Localism with a narrow minded selfish focus. For IfF building a local community does not exclude interaction with the wider world. As Frome town council, we have developed clear directives to contract local firms wherever possible and we also have an ethical policy which extends well beyond the ongoing commitment to being a FairTrade town. This is well illustrated by our using the opportunity presented by the district closing their public toilets. We have developed a community toilet scheme whereby local businesses provide public access to their facilities. In addition five out of eight of these toilets are now twinned with toilets in Africa, built from donations from Frome people and businesses.

> "Maybe the right local questions and answers will be the right global ones. The Amish query, 'What will this do to our community?' may be the important starting point for all of our decisions."
>
> *Mel Usher – councillor*

Although I have systematically panned the district council, throughout this guide, there are areas where we have developed working relationships. Also staff, at both levels, seem to work reasonably well together even if the 'politicians' don't. By a mixture of support and pressure we have vastly increased the funds coming from the district from the '106 agreements' that developers are obliged to put in place for community infrastructure. We also still have hopes for the New Homes Bonus that central government pays to local communities to encourage house building – but so far this is mostly stuck at the district level. Funding sources like these are incredibly important at local level, where the core budget is strictly limited. A competent, motivated town council staff has been crucial in taking advantage of these and other funding opportunities.

I provide these examples in part to return to an earlier point: I believe that local councils – and councillors – can play a key role in enabling communities to increase their resilience to the challenges we increasingly face. If your ambition is to repaint the park benches, to replace the councillor you don't like, or to regale the good people with your political ideology, I suggest your motives are misguided. My case is that there is real potential for individuals to enable change in their communities.

Which brings us to two important questions in relation to whether the 'Frome experience' can work elsewhere:

Question 1: Is what we have achieved in Frome specific to this place and this group of people or can it be replicated?

A number of key issues that worked against the existing town council politicians came together at the time of the election:

Firstly, a recent history of uninspiring Frome town councils. But was Frome especially unimpressive? For every hard working and excellent council there are many others ranging from moribund to deeply dodgy. For people with the misfortune to live in areas governed by the not-so-splendid councils this means, at best, opportunities for local communities are being missed and at worst, their resources are being misused and the future shape of those communities controlled for personal gain. In my view, Frome was more about a waste of opportunity than anything really sinister. This showed itself partly in uncontested seats and councillors appointed without election.

Secondly, a high profile issue involving the proposed takeover of a community building that the existing council had made a very public mess of. This definitely helped IfF to focus, just as 'Open Liskeard' benefitted from what was widely seen as dodgy dealing by councillors. I'd suggest these factors are a help but not essential. Part of the ethos of this guide is to try and create a new way of doing things, rather than looking too hard for things (and parties) to oppose. There is a case to be made that it's better simply not to engage at all with adversarial politics and messaging. It is clear to me that many, many, councils will have made poor decisions that can be used in an Independent's campaigning. However, unless the crimes are particularly heinous, a more positive approach would be to focus on missed opportunities. We used the unpopular issue to get people into a room to launch the 'movement', but never really mentioned it again. So, in my view a high profile negative issue can be a useful catalyst but is far from essential.

Thirdly, national politics at the time badly affected the fortunes of the Liberal Democrats. There is no doubt we gained from a collapse in Liberal Democrat support based on their dismal record in the national coalition. As I write that process of disaffection seems likely to continue, whilst on the right UKIP are likely to pinch more of the Tory vote. If the Independent message is strong enough, it will mobilise voters fed up with party politics. It is unlikely to make a huge impression on the core of people hard wired to support their parties. In other words, our job is to properly engage the electorate, appeal to the disillusioned and to bring in new voters.

In contrast there were several key issues working for the success of IfF:

- We came together as a group of people with enthusiasm for change.
- The group had a reasonably wide range of backgrounds and ages – mostly working professionals.
- A number of our members had a history of engagement and radical thought – not necessarily in politics, but in other areas of social concern.
- Amongst us was an ex-chief executive of a local authority who has considerable local government experience – and who became IfF convenor then council leader.
- And, finally, we supported this core with people with skills in areas including marketing, social media and local government who were prepared to give their time to the IfF challenge.

So, are these conditions unique? Of course Frome and our story is unique, but I don't believe there is anything in the above which argues that our achievements cannot be replicated. There will sometimes be stronger opposition and sometimes fewer resources – and it may take longer. I believe a well built and managed Movement for Change can meet similar objectives without the all the unique features we had.

Question 2: If key elements of IfF's methodology are replicable, are they limited to only smaller councils in the UK?

Here we are in less tested waters. The current situation is that there are Independents at all levels of UK government, though clearly fewer as you go up, with only two Independent MPs since 1950 (and only another eight from minor parties such as the Greens and Respect). Other than these it's all been party politicians.

In 2012, on the lowest electoral turnout in UK peacetime history, 11 out of 41 of the new police and crime commissioners elected were Independents capturing 27% of the votes cast. Similarly the advent of directly elected mayors has brought a clutch of Independents. The first, interestingly enough, was Stuart Drummond in Hartlepool whose only promise was for the council to provide free bananas for school children. Most recently, Independent George Ferguson was elected mayor of Bristol. He is receiving a lot of support for his green agenda. As an aside, the possibility that green policy is more acceptable from Independents than green politicians is an interesting topic that bears further discussion. I suspect there are two elements at work here: an element of anti-politics in relation to the police job; and in the case of the mayors a very British approval of mavericks and self-publicists. In other words, it seems fun voting for a man in a monkey suit for mayor and there is the frisson of excitement that it may all go horribly wrong. In the event, Stuart Drummond went on to be re-elected twice with greatly increased majorities before Hartlepool abolished the mayoral system.

Across all the various options – County, Unitary Authority, District, Assemblies etc – nearly 2000 seats were held by 'Independents and others' after the May 2013 elections (just under 10%). Of those some will be Independents who have resigned from or been thrown out of their parties. Others are 'one issue' people, such as Morley Borough Independents who came together on the sole issue of protecting Morley's greenfield sites. So, very nearly all of these Independents will not be acting together in any pre-agreed way and do not hold power as a group. In my view, although this is solid number of individuals, they are not playing a significant role in changing the dysfunctional system in which they operate. Indeed, most will be marginalised within it as insignificant opposition.

A notable exception is the Isle of Wight which, in May 2013, elected their first wholly Independent council for 40 years. All councillors signed up to the Bell Principles (see chapter 4). As a group they are set on a comprehensive review of all services, are moving from the cabinet style of government and plan for "… constitutional changes that will result in a return to more transparent, accountable and democratic governance for the Island." One of the web comments on the Isle of Wight relating to this reads:

> "My prediction is that within a matter of weeks the Independent group will be fighting like rats in a sack and whoever is charged with trying to keep the group together will be at nervous breakdown point before long…" But does go on to say "… but whatever happens it's going to be better than having the last lot in charge!"

The current situation is that while there are a significant number of non-party councillors at local level, there are few at higher levels of government (with some notable exceptions). And, at the local levels, very few set out to work in a co-ordinated manner in order to achieve greater things.

A key element to the question of scalability at higher levels of government is whether in standing for election you need to make detailed promises related to what you will do once elected? The methodology we used in Frome essentially asked voters to support individuals with a set of values, skills and experience. IfF's candidates have not signed up to a predetermined set of promises on given issues but have said how they will reach decisions and the areas in which we would focus.

At a recent Bristol Big Green Week event – 'Beyond (Party) Politics' – it was clear that the Independents for Bristol had struggled when campaigning with questions about their policy. At that meeting, the Frome model was vigorously rejected by Mayor George Ferguson and Jonathan Porritt (founder of the Ecology Party – the forerunner of the Green Party). They argued that individuals without a manifesto can potentially hide extreme or otherwise unacceptable views. It is certainly true that at higher levels where policy on education, immigration, health, transport etc will be required, then having a view on these is important. It is also true that understanding candidates' views on key issues is the traditional way for a voter to make choices.

However, if we are to create a new form of politics there is a balance we need to move towards. I am unconvinced that setting out policies in great detail prior to election and doggedly sticking to them afterwards, enables sound decision making later, for two reasons:

Firstly, in reality you can't form an opinion without access to information and you really don't get all the information until you are in power. So it is unhelpful to pre-guess at detailed areas of policy and strategy. Secondly, all the evidence is that the predetermined manifesto route has failed us. Elected politicians rarely do what they said they would and usually do things they didn't mention before. In part this is because once in power they find information that makes it impossible to keep promises but it is also because party politicians the world over say what they think the voters may want to hear. Anything goes in order to get elected.

Secondly, most candidates hide behind their manifesto, telling us next to nothing about who they are, their skills, interests and background and how they are likely to behave once in power. This is a huge problem at local level where real relationships with people is going to be more important than a knowledge of complex political issues.

I accept that there will be a need to define broad areas where a group of Independents will focus. We did this in Frome, facilitating a process to reach broad areas of agreement that reflected community priorities. I also accept that this approach presents a significant and unresolved issue for working in higher levels of government. The way we have done things in Frome demands a fundamental change in approach to discussions, to information gathering, and to decision making. It means asking people to trust you. And given that politicians are widely distrusted, this would mean a very significant turnaround! 93% in a September 2013 poll said they have little or no faith in an elected representative to tell the truth.

So, to turn question 2 on its head we should ask: 'Can and should candidates and elected representatives at these higher levels adopt elements of the methodology IfF has chosen?' To which I would say: Definitely. At higher levels of government, will Independents working as a group be electable if they focus on a Way of Working and ethos? On this I am far less clear. However, I remain totally convinced that 'business as usual' is not an option. If those within the system do not seek to change it, in due course those on the streets may well invite them to do so more forcefully.

Afterword.

IfF is definitely a work in progress. It will be some time before we will know if this group of individuals, doing their bit in Frome, have really changed local democracy or have just been an effective group of councillors, guiding a town council to greater than normal achievements for a short period. After four years will others will take our place and the experiment continue? Or will Frome return to a previous age of party political dinosaurs?

The case this guide has set out to make is that by organising as a group outside of party politics, and by operating a Way of Working which is in keeping with natural human behaviour, it is possible to engineer real change to the increasingly divisive mechanisms of government. I believe in localism and the strength and wisdom of communities and that there is potential for new Localism legislation to be used – quite probably not as it was intended. Human nature tends towards cooperation not confrontation – but yet our current systems are based entirely on confrontation. I believe we can engage a public who are deserting democracy in droves. And we must, because if we do not change democracy to a tool that can be used to create a better and more equable society, we risk social breakdown. We must not reject this crucial opportunity to be better prepared for an increasingly challenging period of human history. So, now, over to you.

"Most of us in Frome don't want to be passive consumers, electing distant representatives once every four years to make decisions on our behalf. Many are searching for greater action and collaboration in public life. We want to encourage them, indeed the more the merrier. Why shouldn't Frome people 'do politics', involving themselves in innovative work to help re-energise the town through identifying hyper local issues of concern and making dynamic changes over issues they care about?"

Mel Usher – councillor

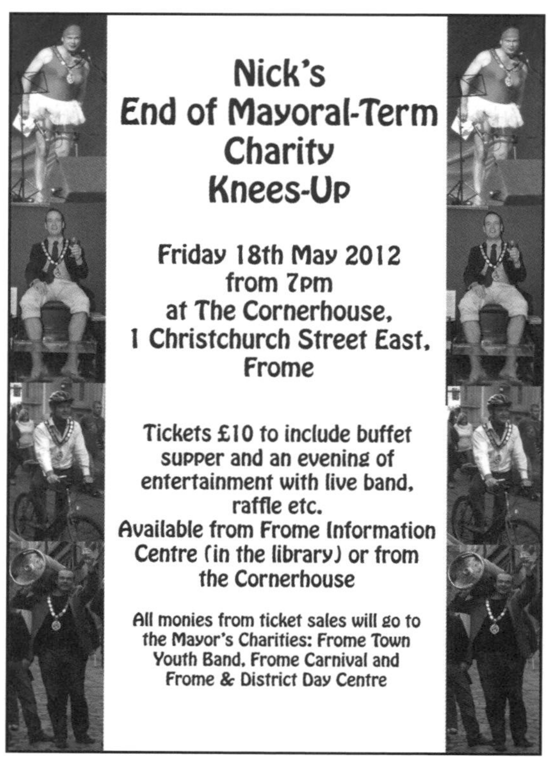

Flyer for Nick White's end of term as mayor charity 'knees up'

Appendix 1 – The People

There were 17 heads that poked above Frome's political parapet. Their personal statements, culled from their own election addresses, can be found below:

The first ten were elected.

Nick White

I don't know if I am cut out for political life, I am not bad at bar room politics but in real life I don't think I have the patience... I am a Frome man in that I was born at the Frome Victoria 49 years ago, attended most of the schools in the town, I then worked at Butler & Tanner (printers) for 26 years... I have a big investment in this town. I love the place and feel very lucky to have lived here most of my life.

Pippa Goldfinger

I am an engineer and mother of two. I am passionate about Frome and the lively mix of people in my neighbourhood. My kids have attended nursery, first school and now attend Middle School in Frome. Frome is great but I can see a growing divide in the town which I would love to bridge. I'm an urban design enthusiast so would love to see better paving, lighting, roads and street furniture.

Peter Macfadyen

I came here 25 years ago to help set up Action on Disability and Development (an International charity); I left them to work for other charities – now mostly Comic Relief. My children were born and educated here. I believe there are almost always opportunities in moments of change and unrest. I believe the town council could, and should, play a central networking role, aggressively promoting and supporting the long term interests of the town's people, through existing groups.

Mel Usher

I started off life as a Sociologist (failed) and Town Planner (equally failed). Variety of senior roles in Local Government. Ran an award winning national agency for Local Government improvement. Now a consultant to public sector and chairman of two small companies and a charity. I would like the council to rethink its role not so much as a provider of services but as a body that can tap into all of the talent in the town and can assist in Frome finding an assertive voice.

Toby Eliot

I've lived in Frome, with my wife and our two sons, since 2003. All four of us are actively involved in different aspects of life in the town. Now is the time to have strong local representation as the current government washes its hands of implementing the detail of throttling public sector cuts handing those decisions to more localised bodies. I work as a Performance and Information Manager for Integrated Youth Services and maintain an interest ensuring young people's rights, responsibilities and involvement. I want to see Frome Town Council and all the councillors stand up for the town's interest when dealing with the higher levels of government: district, county and national.

Dickon Moore

I have lived in Frome for 8 years I would hope to work with the IFF Group on a common strategy in order to better direct progress towards genuinely Frome-centred goals. Since leaving college [in 2010], my main focus has been to involve myself with the Silk Mill Arts project started by my parents in the private sector. I have recently begun to study for an Open University Maths Degree.

Tricia Golinski

I currently work part-time as Parish Clerk in Saltford and am studying for the Certificate in Local Council Administration. I help manage Sustainable Frome's accounts and co-ordinate the Transport Group of Sustainable Frome. I am impressed by the six principles of IFF and would like to participate in a council based on these.

Dave Anderson

I've lived & worked in Frome for 27 years and have been politically apathetic for 26. I have no political knowledge or aspiration, but am passionately against injustice and misrepresentation towards Frome and its residents. I agree with all I.F.F. principles and feel the current 'autocratic policy makers' are completely oblivious to the needs and desires of EVERY Frome citizen. Maybe it's an age thing! I would like to be included in changing Frome, positively, openly & above all, democratically, regardless of personal desires and ideas.

Graham Burgess

I was an Independent district councillor for four years and am currently a self-employed architectural designer. I enjoy reasoned argument and I relish the prospect of engaging with others who also enjoy it, particularly in the cause of helping to facilitate the running of the town I love living in. I'd also be keen to review the organisational structures and methods of operation within the town council – but not so as to sweep them away only to replace them with new untried models – but to make only the smallest changes necessary to effect a positive change. A constant theme in recent TC history seems to have been a misguided (and expensive) drive to acquire status symbols whilst at the same time being seemingly blind to the real home-grown vitality of the place. I want the town council to feed and encourage these combined energies as effectively as possible because it is this energy – not the council – which truly runs the town.

Helen Starkie

I am a solicitor practising on my own account from premises in Bath and also from my home in Frome. My particular area of expertise is law for the older and/or vulnerable client. I do not belong to any political party or group; I do belong to local clubs and societies and my social life centres around Frome. I am a believer in the principle of 'put up or shut up'. I deplore apathy. As a result I have been/am a school governor and trustee of a number of local and national charities. In my capacity as a charity trustee I have experience of lottery funding applications. It is my view that politics should not govern local issues. Local issue should inform politics.

It is Frome's loss that the following were not elected (this time).

Dave Clark

I have lived in Frome for the last 10 years. I love this town and feel very much at home here, having lived in many other parts of the UK. It seems quite clear to me that our generation bears a very special responsibility to do what it can and must to mitigate with some urgency the effects of human activity on our planet. We do not have the luxury of leaving what must be done to future generations. To safeguard the uniqueness of this town, Frome needs to speak with a strong voice at district, county and national levels. Frome has the potential to be an inspiration, a good example. I have no previous experience of local politics and don't particularly feel like getting entangled in the arcane intricacies of small town bureaucracy...

John Birkett-Smith.

I moved to Frome in 1987. Both children went through Frome schools, then on to university. I trained and worked as an architect and planner in London then with my wife, bought Hunting Raven Books in Cheap Street in 2000; we have run it since then. I was a Frome town vouncillor from 1990-2003 (with a four year gap).

Richard Porteous

I served for eight years on Frome Town Council as a Labour councillor, but left the party in 2003 following the invasion of Iraq and have been quite content to stay at home and witness local affairs from the fireside ever since. I have experienced the corrosive nature of party politics within local government and the Yah Boo style of debate that results from power through simple arithmetic majorities. The time is now right for a complete overhaul of Frome Town Council and all of its systems. The thought of an experienced, intelligent, rational, active, open, sustainable and truly independent Council being in control is extremely exciting and is something I wish to be a part of.

Sue Klepper

The time seems right now for citizens' initiatives – doing something at a community level for the common good, not necessarily influenced by party views. Cuts at the moment seem to be about withdrawing funding from as many things as possible – hoping that charity and volunteers will take over. I am particularly interested in projects for older people.

Pip Utton

For too long I have been content to moan, sometimes loudly, about national and local government. I moan about their out of date, out of touch ways of conducting business, and I moan about the unbreakable slavish obedience to the party line; whichever party. So it's time for me to stop moaning, get off my lazy backside and put my time and effort where my mouth is. I would want to examine and reform the way the town council works making the decision making process as rigorous, open and transparent as possible. I am Vice Chair of Edinburgh Festival Fringe and an actor/write whose work has been translated into five languages, and who performs around the world.

Clare Tayler

I have been living in and around Frome for the past 15 years. I have never been one for sitting back and just taking things lying down… with a number of weird and wonderfully curious decisions made by the local council in recent years, I feel compelled to do something about it. I currently work four days a week as a Practice Manager at NVB Architects. Good communication is usually the swiftest way to resolving most issues. I am somewhat nervous of any campaign publicity etc., as it is more the background and getting things done that I am interested in, but I guess it is the nature of the beast.

Charlie Thomas

I have lived in Frome for the majority of the last 15 years, going to school at Selwood and Frome College. After frequent trips to Nicaragua and a few years completing a degree in photography at Arts Institute Bournemouth, I moved back to Frome. I worked for two years at the Griffin pub in Milk Street as manager, before I began managing St. Catherine's Artisan Market and became general manager at Black Swan Arts.

Appendix 2 – IfF Ambition

The list below is shared to support the notion of aspiration. Hopefully it will inspire people to stand as local councillors and to gain power because it is possible to create significant positive change – driven by an ethos and a focus on the community and not party politics.

I cannot prove that all the items below were 'our idea' or might not have happened anyway. However the fact is they have occurred during IfF's first few years of tenure and they had not happened before. Come to think of it, no one seems to remember much of any significance that did happen back then.

The Council

Completely revamped the committee and officer structure of the council. Improving effectiveness and morale without significant extra cost. Finalising plans to move the town council offices to the Library, saving money and securing its future. Becoming a 'forerunner' in preparing a draft Neighbourhood Plan so that the town can now have more say and control in planning and development.

Town Centre

Prepared a £2m Heritage Lottery Bid for Town Centre Regeneration alongside major 106 funding from a supermarket extension (to 'compensate' the community for additional costs). This plan is based on extensive consultation and expert inputs designed to meet the number one need, as expressed by Frome residents, for better movement and use of the town centre. We had a key role in establishing the 'Frome Super Market' which now runs every month attracting many local businesses and thousands of visitors.

Further 106 development money

The council has persuaded, encouraged and supported the district to ensure significant sums of money previously agreed and not collected, or currently in negotiation, have been made available for projects in the town. (In January 2014 there was £1.5Bn 106 money held by English councils and not spent.)

Poverty

Establishing a trust to secure £150k of private funds to open a Resource and Resilience Centre for struggling families and individuals. This centre will work with a range of agencies and organisations, such as the credit union, food bank and family unit, to focus on meeting real needs.

River Frome Corridor Project

Completing a community led feasibility study; funding a circular walk; purchasing a meadow in central Frome to add to community space; carrying out works with local youngsters in partnership with a local training agency. This includes working with a voluntary organisation to attract lottery funding and build an amazingly successful BMX bike track.

Cheese and Grain building

By borrowing and investing £500,000 in this community building, it has gone from needing an annual subsidy to a commercial venture (at significantly less cost to the town each year). The venue has moved from just a music venue to a hub for youth issues. These include employing local apprentices, working with the college on practical music skills, a new bar/café/incubation centre open all week and self-financing. By investing £30K in installing photovoltaic cells these now generate a £6k+ return per year together with free electricity for the building.

Allotments

Negotiating the purchase of land (60% with a private donation) for 100 new allotments, a community meadow and orchard, massively reducing the ten year waiting list. In parallel transferred ownership and management of all allotments to the Allotments Association. Further extensive land acquisition from areas which had been held by the district and left in a state of neglect. Followed by careful and detailed consultation to agree usage and management of these areas by and for local residents.

Saxonvale

Purchasing land adjacent to a large ex-industrial area and through this securing training for 1,500 youngsters a year.

Investment in the Voluntary Sector

IfF councillors were instrumental in setting up Frome Community Interest Company funded with £50k pa by a local trust tasked with 'oiling wheels' at a local level for worthy causes. In parallel, the council increased grants to the voluntary sector to £100k pa including People's Grant of 10k voted on by local people; the contracting of professional advisors to help local groups make Lottery and other grant applications; and funding to support the establishment of a network of loyal organisations.

Energy

The town council commissioned a report on the potential for renewable energy generation in Frome. This included an online resource that can be used to share data and ideas on renewable energy generation with the community. The Town's new Energy and Waste Officer will work closely with Frome Renewable Energy Co-op (FRECo) – a new community energy company that has been established to deliver renewable energy projects in and around Frome.

Youth

Detailed research has been carried out to identify exactly how best to support young people. Working in partnership with the County and the YMCA and utilising the knowledge of the town's new Mayor for Young People and her deputy.

Frome as a place that says 'Yes'

All of the above have raised the profile of Frome as a place where things happen. Significant publicity about the good things and the spirit of Frome has been generated not least by attracting former racing car world champion Jenson Button to turn on the Christmas lights before driving (fast) through the town. The council made film of event which has attracted hundreds of thousands of Internet views. A quick visit to the Frome Town Council website or Vimeo and a search under 'Frome Jenson Button' will give you a flavour of the event.

The above is not an exhaustive list. It aims to provide a few examples of how a well-led, dynamic council, with councillors focussed only on their town, can do more than footle with bus shelters and dog mess.

Appendix 3 – Facilitation

I maintain that it is an ESSENTIAL to use skilled facilitation to form a group of Independents. Just as the leaders of a group cannot conduct a process of consultation themselves – because they will have their own views which will either dominate or end up not being expressed. One of the challenges facing IfF in the beginning was to be clear about what bound us together as a coherent group, when, by definition, we are all independently minded individuals. In order to address this issue we used a facilitator who guided us through the challenges thrown up by this apparent paradox. The result was the recognition that, though individually we have a range of views, collectively we wanted to conduct ourselves in a respectful, open and positive way. The initial focus was on 'how' not 'what'. These facilitated discussions drew heavily on methods developed by the Institute of Cultural Affairs (**www.ica-uk.org**), an organisation concerned with helping communities bring about positive change through partnership and participation. They have a particular expertise in developing and using consensus building methods in their work.

IfF's desire to focus on the positive aspects of the town, its people and the way it conducted politics was reinforced by a process known as 'Appreciative Inquiry' which seeks to discover the best in communities. With the support of a facilitator, IfF used this approach to help develop a vision and guide us in how to put our message out to the community. To find out more about this approach see *The Appreciative Inquiry Handbook* by Cooperrider, Whitney and Stavros. Published by Berrett-Koehler, 2005.

Here are two of the Appreciative Inquiry Methods:

1. The Award Ceremony

- Ask people to imagine their town council has just won an award for the most innovative and progressive town council in England.
- Divide into four groups and ask each group to prepare an acceptance speech from the perspective of:
    - The Chamber of Commerce
    - The public
    - A voluntary organisation
    - Council employees
- Each group delivers their speeches
- The facilitator draws out and writes on flipchart paper all the visionary elements of the speeches forming a basis for the council's vision.
- If this is what we want people to say about us, what are the first steps in achieving this?

There may be other groups you may wish to include in the above categories e.g. a local school, the Civic Society etc. I would suggest no more than four.

2. The Consensus Building Method

- Prepare a question you would like to focus on. The question needs to be unambiguous and simple eg 'What are the essential ingredients of a successful independent council?'
- Ask individuals to write down on a piece of paper whatever comes to mind in answer to the question, and tell them there are no right or wrong answers.
- Divide the group into pairs or small groups. You don't want more than six groups, so if there are 12 people you need 6 pairs; if there are 30 people then you need 6 groups of 5.
- Ask each individual to read out their answers to their partner/other group members.
- Notice the differences and similarities, and then combine your answers so that you come up with six distinct answers.
- Write your answers on a large post-it note, ensuring that each answer is no more than five words and contains one concept only.
- Ask each group to pick out their top three. The facilitator then collects these and displays them on a wall or board at random, reading them out loud as they go on the wall.
- Ask the group to see if any match or say the same thing and put these together. Don't worry if some answers don't match.
- When this process is complete, ask if any of the remaining answers match any of those displayed and place them on the wall next to them.
- If there is any disagreement, let the discussion flow. If after a few minutes there is still disagreement, go back to the group that came up with the answer in the first place and let them have the final say.
- When all answers are displayed and in columns, begin to name each column in such a way that it answers the original question. So, for example one column may be headed 'open and honest communication'.
- You should end up with no more than eight or nine columns.
- Read out the question and all the answers.

You will end up with an answer that everyone has been involved with and will form the basis of the next stage in your groups plan.

An example – from minutes of an early IfF meeting:

Part One. Getting to know each other and working out the issues

After ascertaining that all the candidates were eligible to stand for town council, Mel gave a short introduction outlining some of the problems that they may face as a group of Independents. After everyone had introduced themselves, Neil Oliver, our facilitator, then led a session in groups to discuss the question: "What are the essential ingredients of a successful independent political movement?"

Each group then identified seven issues which they thought were important. These issues were then honed down and clarified by the meeting to produce eight common core issues which everyone agreed were essential ingredients. They were:

- To identify and act on issues.
- A commitment to the task and each other.
- To create and maintain excitement over time.
- To be able to engage with the people of Frome.
- To be honest and open (both internally and externally).
- To trust each other and the people we serve.
- To be clear in all communications.
- To know when to stop!

Part Two. The campaign

Groups were identified for different aspects of the work and filled with volunteers as follows:

Coordination: Peter M, Helen, John, Mel.

Leaflets: Nick, Dickon, Dave C, Tricia, Clare.

Website: Dickon, Charlie, Toby, Peter (initially).

Boards and Households: Graham, John, Mike, Richard.

Media strategy: Sue, Pippa, Pip, Charlie.
Wacky ideas: Clare, Pippa, Dave C, Peter, Charlie.

Matters raised:

- Families, friends and supporters need to be rallied for leafleting.
- Distribution of leaflets on market days as well as door.
- Canvassing to be undertaken where candidates feel comfortable and have the time.
- IfF will deal with all the registration documents so that candidates don't have to do it on their own.
- It was suggested that candidates should go to town council meetings leading up to the election to see and be seen.

The facilitator IfF used was Neil Oliver. He is happy to be contacted through his company, The Oliver Barclay Partnership, for more information or possible support.

Appendix 4 – Localism

The IfF ethos can be made to work in part because of new legislation aimed at giving more power at a local level – understanding these powers is crucial.

The information IfF provided on our website on localism:
Independents for Frome is a movement, not a political party. We don't just put people up for election to the town council; we want to see the community make its own decisions for the future of the town. And we want your help!

To this end we're looking closely at the new Localism Act and those powers that are now available to a town like Frome. We need to understand these powers and use them responsibly but they provide opportunities for Frome to break away from the shackles of decisions made elsewhere and in the interests of others.

The Government have introduced four 'Community Rights'
Community Right to Build – giving communities the right to build small-scale, site-specific projects without planning permission
Neighbourhood Planning – giving communities more say about what can be built in their area
Community Right to Challenge – giving communities the right to challenge to take over a council service they think they can run differently or better
Community Right to Bid – giving communities the right to bid to buy and take over the running of local assets that are important to them

More detail can be found on the Community Rights web site (search for 'My Community Rights').

More detail on the Localism Act.

The Localism Act, introduced in 2010 and passed in November 2011, was conceived to fulfil the Government's stated commitment to decentralising control over public services, assets and planning from central government to local government and from local government to communities. The Localism Act contains measures which pertain to dozens of areas, including housing, planning, local services, and local governance structures. One of these areas is the Community Rights agenda, which includes the Community Right to Bid, Community Right to Challenge and Community Right to Build. The Government believes that for too long local communities have been prevented from doing things for themselves because of cumbersome local authority processes and too much red tape. Community Rights were conceived to address this issue, giving communities explicit powers in the areas of local assets, local services, planning and developing

There are four Community Rights. The new Rights contained within the Localism Act came into effect in 2012 devolving power from government to communities, local authorities and individuals.

Full details can be found on the web, search for '**My Community Rights**' site. A brief summary of the main sections follows:

Community Right to Build.

The Right to Build gives communities the power to build new shops, housing or community facilities without going through the normal planning process. In the context of the localism agenda, Neighbourhood Planning and the Community Right to Build are the initiatives introduced which aim to decentralise power over planning directly into the hands of local communities and cut red tape for areas that wish to encourage local development.

Neighbourhood Planning.

This allows local areas to come together to establish general planning policies for development and use of land in their neighbourhood, which then becomes part of the local plan. Neighbourhood plans already exist in some areas, usually called 'parish plans', but the Localism Act makes neighbourhood plans part of the legal framework. The Community Right to Build goes hand in hand with this process and allows a community to draw up a Community Right to Build Order which, if supported in a local referendum, enables small local development to go ahead without going through the normal planning application process.

Community Right to Bid

The Right to Bid gives communities the opportunity to bid to buy and run valued local amenities if they come onto the open market. The Government has aimed to address concerns that too often local buildings and land that are of great value to the community, such as a village hall or local pub, go up for sale and are purchased by a private bidder before the community has the opportunity to put together funding and take it over themselves. The Community Right to Bid gives communities the power to submit assets of community value to be kept on a list by the local authority. If any of these buildings or land are put up for sale, a six week window of opportunity is triggered during which the community group may express an interest to purchase the asset. If they do express an interest, a further four and a half month window of opportunity is given so that the group may have time to find funding and put together a bid to purchase the asset on the open market.

Community Right to Challenge.

The Right to Challenge gives local groups the opportunity to express their interest in taking over a local service where they think they can do it differently and better. The Community Right to Challenge aims to help communities bid to take over local authority and fire and rescue authority services that they feel they could run better or differently on behalf of the authority. If a community group, charity, parish council or group of staff is able to identify a service that they would like to run, the Community Right to Challenge gives them the power to submit an expression of interest to the authority to take it over. If the local authority accepts the expression of interest, they must run a competitive procurement exercise for the service which the interested group takes part in.

Sadly, the reality of the Localism Act has so far turned out not to offer all the opportunities it might have done, particularly at parish level because it turns out 'local' is often taken to mean 'district' – where in our experience ideas and ambition stall, and resources (i.e. money) get siphoned off. *The Flatpack Democracy* blog includes a particularly insightful article by Mel Usher from a presentation to the South West Localism Group in December 2013.